First World War
and Army of Occupation
War Diary
France, Belgium and Germany

21 DIVISION
110 Infantry Brigade
Leicestershire Regiment
8th Battalion
1 July 1916 - 31 May 1918

WO95/2165/1

The Naval & Military Press Ltd
www.nmarchive.com
Published in association with The National Archives

Published by

The Naval & Military Press Ltd

Unit 10 Ridgewood Industrial Park,

Uckfield, East Sussex,

TN22 5QE England

Tel: +44 (0) 1825 749494

www.naval-military-press.com

www.nmarchive.com

This diary has been reprinted in facsimile from the original. Any imperfections are inevitably reproduced and the quality may fall short of modern type and cartographic standards.

Contents

Document type	Place/Title	Date From	Date To
Heading	WO95/2165/1		
Heading	21st Division 110th Infy Bde 8th Bn Leicester Regt Jly 1916-May 1918 From 37 Div To 25 Div and returned to U.K.		
Heading	110th Inf. Bde. 21st Div. War Diary 8th Battn. The Leicestershire Regiment July 1916 May 18		
War Diary	Billets La Cauchie	01/07/1916	04/07/1916
War Diary	Hillbulamps	05/07/1916	06/07/1916
War Diary	Talmas	06/07/1916	07/07/1916
War Diary	Soues	08/07/1916	21/07/1916
War Diary	Longpre	22/07/1916	23/07/1916
War Diary	Gouy Au Trenches	24/07/1916	24/07/1916
War Diary	Lattre St. Quentin	25/07/1916	27/07/1916
War Diary	Arras	28/07/1916	28/07/1916
War Diary	Trenches (98-101)	29/07/1916	31/07/1916
Miscellaneous	Appendices		
Operation(al) Order(s)	110th Brigade Operation Order No. 28 July 13th 1916	13/07/1916	13/07/1916
Miscellaneous	110th Inf Bde. 21st Bn G 50	12/07/1916	12/07/1916
Operation(al) Order(s)	21 Div. O.O. No. 60	11/07/1916	11/07/1916
Miscellaneous	110 Inf. Bde. 5 Copies.	13/07/1916	13/07/1916
Miscellaneous	62nd Inf. Bde. 5	11/07/1916	11/07/1916
Miscellaneous	21 Div. G. 90	11/07/1916	11/07/1916
Miscellaneous	21 Div. G. 90.	13/07/1916	13/07/1916
Operation(al) Order(s)	21 Div. O.O. No. 61	18/07/1916	18/07/1916
Miscellaneous	Divisional Orders With Reference To Improvement OF Positions.		
Miscellaneous	XV Corps Summary Of Information	15/07/1916	15/07/1916
Miscellaneous	8th-Leicester		
Miscellaneous	Units Identified By Prisoners Taken During Advance On German Second Line.		
Miscellaneous	Examination Of Prisoners.	13/07/1916	13/07/1916
Miscellaneous			
Miscellaneous	Examination Of Prisoner Max Borus, Sanitaetseldat, Captured On Morning 12th July In Mametz Wood.	13/07/1916	13/07/1916
Miscellaneous	8th-Leicesters		
Miscellaneous	Prisoners Captured Today By The XV Corps As Follows.	14/07/1916	14/07/1916
Miscellaneous	Prisoners Captured Today By The XV Corps As Follows.	15/07/1916	15/07/1916
Miscellaneous	XV Corps Intelligence Summary Covering The Period From 7.30 P.m. The 15th inst to 7.30 p.m. the 16th inst.	16/07/1916	16/07/1916
Miscellaneous	XV Corps Summary Of Information.	16/07/1916	16/07/1916
Miscellaneous	8th Leic Rg		
Miscellaneous	Translation Of Documents	16/07/1916	16/07/1916
Miscellaneous	XV Corps Daily Intelligence Summary Covering the period from 7.30 p.m. 16th inst to 7.30 p.m. the 17th inst.	17/07/1916	17/07/1916
Miscellaneous	Copy Of G.H.Q. No. O.A.D. 69	15/07/1916	15/07/1916
Miscellaneous	Special Order by Major-General D.G.M. Campbell, C.B. Comdg. 21st Division.	18/07/1916	18/07/1916

Heading	For War Diary		
Miscellaneous	Fourth Army No. 266 (G). 21st Division.	21/07/1916	21/07/1916
Miscellaneous			
Operation(al) Order(s)	110th Infantry Brigade Operation Order No. 29	26/07/1916	26/07/1916
Operation(al) Order(s)	6th (Service) Battalion Of Cornwall's Light Infantry.	27/07/1916	27/07/1916
Miscellaneous	Maps		
Map	Montauban		
Miscellaneous	Montauban		
Map	Area Of Martinpuich		
Miscellaneous	Trench map Area of Martinpuich		
Heading	110th Brigade 21st Division. 1/8th Battalion Leicestershire Regiment August 1916		
War Diary	Trenches (98-101)	01/08/1916	07/08/1916
War Diary	Agnel-Les-Duisans	08/08/1916	17/08/1916
War Diary	Trenches (99-101)	18/08/1916	31/08/1916
Miscellaneous	Relief Orders.	02/08/1916	02/08/1916
Operation(al) Order(s)	Operation Order No. 39 By Major G.C.I. Hervey, Commdg., 8th (Ser) Bn. Leicestershire Regt.	06/08/1916	06/08/1916
Miscellaneous	Special Tasks For Ensuing Week	19/08/1916	19/08/1916
Heading	110th Brigade. 21st Division. 1/8th Battalion Leicestershire Regiment September 1916		
War Diary	Trenches Arras. Sector (98-101)	01/09/1916	05/09/1916
War Diary	Lignereuil	06/09/1916	30/09/1916
War Diary		17/10/1916	31/10/1916
War Diary	Bernafay Wood	01/10/1916	01/10/1916
War Diary	Dernancourt	02/10/1916	04/10/1916
War Diary	Pont Remy	05/10/1916	08/10/1916
War Diary	Fouquereuil	09/10/1916	10/10/1916
War Diary	Hohenzollern Reserve Sector of Trenches	11/10/1916	21/10/1916
War Diary	Support Trenches	22/10/1916	29/10/1916
War Diary	Hohenzollern Sector Of Trenches	30/10/1916	08/11/1916
War Diary	Reserve Sector Of Trenches Hohenzollern	09/11/1916	09/11/1916
War Diary	Front Line Sector Of Trenches	10/11/1916	11/11/1916
War Diary	Hohenzollern Sector Trenches Front line	12/11/1916	15/11/1916
War Diary	Support Line Hohenzollen Sector	16/11/1916	22/11/1916
War Diary	Front Line Hohenzallon Sector Of Trenches	23/11/1916	26/11/1916
War Diary	Hohenzollern Sector Trenches Reserve Line	27/11/1916	30/11/1916
War Diary	Hohenzollern Sector Of Trenches Reserve Line	01/12/1916	03/12/1916
War Diary	Front Line Hohenzallon Sector Of Trenches	03/12/1916	04/12/1916
War Diary	Front Line Hohenzallon Sector	04/12/1916	08/12/1916
War Diary	Hohenzollern Sector Of Trenches Front Line	08/12/1916	10/12/1916
War Diary	Support Trenches Holengollein Sector	11/12/1916	15/12/1916
War Diary	Bethune	16/12/1916	20/12/1916
War Diary	Auehel	21/12/1916	31/12/1916
Miscellaneous	Operation Orders By Major T.L. Warner Comndg. 8th. (Ser) Bn. Leicestershire Regt.	02/12/1916	02/12/1916
Miscellaneous	Distribution		
Miscellaneous	Work Report Of The 8th (Ser) Battn. Leicestershire Regt. From Noon 1-12-16 Noon 8-12-16	01/12/1916	01/12/1916
Miscellaneous	Operation Orders By Lt. Col. H.L. Beardsley, Comndg. 8th, (Ser) Battn. Leicestershire Regt.	08/12/1916	08/12/1916
Miscellaneous	Operation Orders By Lt. Col. H.L. Beardsley. Comndg. 8th. (Ser) Battn. Leicestershire Regt.	14/12/1916	14/12/1916
Miscellaneous	Operation Orders By Lt. Col. H.L. Beardsley, Comndg. 8th. (Ser) Bn. Leicestershire Regt.	19/12/1916	19/12/1916
War Diary	Auchel	01/01/1917	29/01/1917

War Diary	Winnezeele	29/01/1917	31/01/1917
Miscellaneous	8th (SER.) Bn. Leicestershire Regt.	27/01/1917	27/01/1917
Miscellaneous	110th Infantry Brigade	04/01/1917	04/01/1917
War Diary	Winnezeele	01/02/1917	28/02/1917
Operation(al) Order(s)	Operation Orders No. 51. By Lt. Col. C.C.I. Hervey Comndg. 8th. (Ser) Battn. Leicestershire Regt.	12/02/1917	12/02/1917
Operation(al) Order(s)	Operation Orders No. 53. By Lt. Col. C.C.I. Hervey Comndg. 8th. (Ser) Battn. Leicestershire Regt.		
Operation(al) Order(s)	Operation Orders No. 54. By Lt. Col. C.C.I. Hervey Comndg. 8th. (Ser) Battn. Leicestershire Regt.		
Operation(al) Order(s)	Operation Orders No. 56. By Lt. Col. C.C.I. Hervey Comndg. 8th. (Ser) Battn. Leicestershire Regt.	23/02/1917	23/02/1917
Operation(al) Order(s)	Operation Orders No. 55. By Lt. Col. C.C.I. Hervey Comndg. 8th. (Ser) Battn. Leicestershire Regt.	26/02/1917	26/02/1917
War Diary		01/03/1917	31/03/1917
War Diary	La Heshine	01/04/1917	14/04/1917
War Diary	Bailleulmont	15/04/1917	29/04/1917
War Diary	Boyelles	01/05/1917	04/05/1917
War Diary	St. Leger	08/05/1917	09/05/1917
War Diary	Berles Au Bois	11/05/1917	28/05/1917
War Diary	Hamelin Court	01/06/1917	07/06/1917
War Diary	Eroisilles	11/06/1917	19/06/1917
War Diary	Hamelin Court	19/06/1917	19/06/1917
War Diary	Blairville	21/06/1917	01/07/1917
War Diary	Vicinity Of Croisilles	08/07/1917	08/07/1917
War Diary	Grant Line	14/07/1917	14/07/1917
War Diary	Vicinity Of Croisilles	20/07/1917	20/07/1917
War Diary	Front Line	26/07/1917	31/07/1917
War Diary	Moyenville	01/08/1917	01/08/1917
War Diary	Forward Area	09/08/1917	09/08/1917
War Diary	Ervillers	17/08/1917	17/08/1917
War Diary	Barly SE Of Avesnes Le. Comte	25/08/1917	25/08/1917
War Diary	Barly	25/08/1917	25/08/1917
War Diary	Ambrines	26/08/1917	01/09/1917
War Diary	Avesnes-Le-Comte	04/09/1917	04/09/1917
War Diary	Chestre	16/09/1917	16/09/1917
War Diary	Meteren	23/09/1917	23/09/1917
War Diary	St Aubertushuek H.32. C. 3.4	26/09/1917	26/09/1917
War Diary	Ridge Wood H.35.C. 9.3	29/09/1917	30/09/1917
War Diary	Front Line	01/10/1917	02/10/1917
War Diary	Scottish Wood (H. 35.d. Central) (Sheet 28)	02/10/1917	04/10/1917
War Diary	Railway Dugouts Zillebeke I. 21.d.	05/10/1917	08/10/1917
War Diary	Anzac Camp H. 30.c. 5.3 (Sheet 28)	11/10/1917	11/10/1917
War Diary	Le Croquet (Hasenbruck 54)	12/10/1917	12/10/1917
War Diary	Camp At. H. 36 A. 6 7	15/10/1917	22/10/1917
War Diary	Camp A. H. 10. 6. 4.5	23/10/1917	28/10/1917
War Diary	Support & The Front Line	28/10/1917	28/10/1917
War Diary	Railway Dugouts Zillebeke	29/10/1917	31/10/1917
War Diary	Zillebeke	01/10/1917	31/10/1917
War Diary	Clapham Junction	01/10/1917	02/10/1917
War Diary	Zillebeke Lake	03/10/1917	04/10/1917
War Diary	Front Line	04/10/1917	05/10/1917
War Diary	Clapham Junction	05/10/1917	05/10/1917
War Diary	Camp "A"	09/11/1917	09/11/1917
War Diary	Zillebeke Bund	11/11/1917	12/11/1917
War Diary	Front Line	14/11/1917	15/11/1917

War Diary	Zillebeke Bund	16/11/1917	16/11/1917
War Diary	Scottish Wood Area	17/11/1917	17/11/1917
War Diary	Reninghelst Area	18/11/1918	18/11/1918
War Diary	La Bercque	19/11/1917	19/11/1917
War Diary	Arrewage	20/11/1917	20/11/1917
War Diary	Bellerive	21/11/1917	21/11/1917
War Diary	Coupigne	22/11/1917	25/11/1917
War Diary	Monchy Bretton Area	20/11/1917	30/11/1917
War Diary	In The Field	01/12/1917	01/12/1917
War Diary	Support Line	02/12/1917	02/12/1917
War Diary	Front Line	03/12/1917	03/12/1917
War Diary	Bde Reserve	08/12/1917	08/12/1917
War Diary	Front Line	12/12/1917	12/12/1917
War Diary	Support Line	16/12/1917	16/12/1917
War Diary	Front Line	20/12/1917	20/12/1917
War Diary	Saul Court	24/12/1917	24/12/1917
War Diary	Front Line	28/12/1917	28/12/1917
Miscellaneous	Appendix to War Diary For the month of December 1917. 8th Bn. The Leicestershire Regiment		
War Diary	Support (Epehy)	01/01/1918	04/01/1918
War Diary	Middlesex Camp Heudecourt	04/01/1918	04/01/1918
War Diary	Haut Allaines	11/01/1918	11/01/1918
War Diary	Saul Court	16/01/1918	16/01/1918
War Diary	Front Line	20/01/1918	20/01/1918
War Diary	Saul Court (Reserve)	21/01/1918	21/01/1918
War Diary	Front Line	28/01/1918	02/02/1918
War Diary	Support (Epehy)	05/02/1918	05/02/1918
War Diary	Front Line	09/02/1918	09/02/1918
War Diary	York Camp Moislains	15/02/1918	19/02/1918
War Diary	A Camp Gurlu Wood	24/02/1918	24/02/1918
War Diary	Devon Camp Heudecourt	28/02/1918	28/02/1918
Heading	110th Inf. Bde. 21st Div. War Diary 8th Battn. The Leicestershire Regiment. March 1918		
War Diary	Front Line E & Eteny B 6	01/03/1918	01/03/1918
War Diary	Epehy B.6	04/03/1918	04/03/1918
War Diary	Front Line E Of Epehy B. 6	08/03/1918	08/03/1918
War Diary	Epehy B.6	12/03/1918	12/03/1918
War Diary	Front Line E Of Epehy B. 6	17/03/1918	17/03/1918
War Diary	Epehy Alecourt Halt. Green Line	22/03/1918	23/03/1918
War Diary	Green Line E. Of Templeux La Fosse (A.I)	23/03/1918	23/03/1918
War Diary	N.E. Of Clery Sur Somme Mhurevas Bray Sur Summe	24/03/1918	24/03/1918
War Diary	Bray Sur Somme Chipilly	25/03/1918	25/03/1918
War Diary	Chipilly Bresle	26/03/1918	26/03/1918
War Diary	Bresle Vadencourt	27/03/1918	29/03/1918
War Diary	Allonville	30/03/1918	31/03/1918
Miscellaneous	Copy Letter From A.J. Fletcher. I.O. 8th Bn. Leicestershire Regiment. The Fog-March 21st 1918		
Heading	110th Brigade Attcd. 21st Division 1/8th Battalion Leicestershire Regiment April 1918		
War Diary	Allonville	01/04/1918	01/04/1918
War Diary	Poperinghe	02/04/1918	02/04/1918
War Diary	Dranoutre	04/04/1918	04/04/1918
War Diary	Kemmel Chelters	07/04/1918	07/04/1918
War Diary	Curragh Camp	05/04/1918	05/04/1918
War Diary	Ontario Camp	09/04/1918	09/04/1918
War Diary	Manawatu Camp	10/04/1918	10/04/1918

War Diary	Canada Tunnels	13/04/1918	13/04/1918
War Diary	Torr Top	15/04/1918	15/04/1918
War Diary	G.N. Q.I. Livs. Of Prenchis	15/04/1918	15/04/1918
War Diary	Hrar Busse Boom	01/05/1918	01/05/1918
War Diary	Bois De Beauvoorde	02/05/1918	02/05/1918
War Diary	Buysscheure	05/05/1918	05/05/1918
War Diary	In The Train	06/05/1918	06/05/1918
War Diary	Aougny	13/05/1918	13/05/1918
War Diary	Pevy	14/05/1918	14/05/1918
War Diary	Chalons De Vergeur	20/05/1918	20/05/1918
War Diary	Front Line	26/06/1918	26/06/1918
War Diary	Pourcy	30/05/1918	30/05/1918
War Diary	Foret Depernay	31/05/1918	31/05/1918

21ST DIVISION
110TH INFY BDE

8TH BN LEICESTER REGT

JLY 1916-MAY 1918

FROM 37 DIV

TO 25 DIV and [illegible] to UK

DISBANDED 3 7 18

110th Inf.Bde.
21st Div.

WAR DIARY

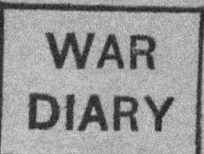

8th BATTN. THE LEICESTERSHIRE REGIMENT.

J U L Y

1 9 1 6

/
May '18

Attached:

Appendices.
Maps.

Instructions regarding War Diaries and Intelligence Summaries are contained in F. S. Regs., Part II. and the Staff Manual respectively. Title Pages will be prepared in manuscript.

WAR DIARY
or
INTELLIGENCE SUMMARY

(Erase heading not required.) 8th (Ser) Batt Leicestershire Regt.

Army Form C. 2118.

16

Place	Date	Hour	Summary of Events and Information	Remarks and references to Appendices
1-7-16. Billets La Cauchie			Parades under Company arrangements. Bn Raiders, Signallers, and Range Finders under their respective officers AAA	
2-7-16.			Comp. S. M. Webb having been granted a temporary commission as 2nd Lt was posted to 7th (S) Bn Lincolnshire Rgt and accordingly struck off our strength AAA Parades as for yesterday AAA	
3-7-16.			The C.O held an inspection of the whole Battalion on their various parade grounds Companies paraded as usual.	
4-7-16			Company parades as usual AAA Specialists under their various officers	
5-7-16. Humbercamps			The Battalion left billets at LA CAUCHIE at 9 am. and arrived at HUMBERCAMPS at 10-30am ~~AAA~~ where we were billeted in huts, some of which had roofs, the Remainder having either no roofs at all or were covered with canvas which would not withstand the rain, and as the weather was exceedingly inclement, most of the men got wet through AAA The men slept in puttees and boots, as we were 'standing to'. In the afternoon the Battn went for a route march by way of St AMAND and GAUDIEMPRE	
6-7-16			The Battn. left billets at HUMBERCAMPS at 12.45 pm, and marched to TALMAS by way of PAS and MARIEUX, a distance of about 18 miles, arriving at TALMAS about 9.30 pm AAA The order of the march was Signallers, A. B. C D Coys AAA. On arrival at PAS we were delighted to find the Divisional band awaiting us, and they helped us considerably on our journey by playing to us for about 5 miles AAA Owing to ~~the~~ weary time in the trenches the men	

Instructions regarding War Diaries and Intelligence Summaries are contained in F. S. Regs., Part II. and the Staff Manual respectively. Title Pages will be prepared in manuscript.

WAR DIARY
or
INTELLIGENCE SUMMARY
(Erase heading not required.) 8 (Ser) Notts Regiment [illegible]

Army Form C. 2118.

17

Place	Date	Hour	Summary of Events and Information	Remarks and references to Appendices
6-7-16 TALMAS.			men had got quite out of condition and it was only by the strenuous exertions of our ~~[illegible]~~ kind and beloved colonel, that enabled us to reach our destination at TALMAS with practically the whole Battalion AAA We arrived at TALMAS about 9.30 pm where we billeted for the night.	
7-7-16			After a sick parade which was held at 7 am. the Battn fell in at 9 am to continue the march, en route for SOUES at distance of about 18 miles AAA Order of march Signallers, D. B. C. A. Coys AAA The 8th Battn led the 110th Inf Bde by way of Vignacourt and Bourdon AAA Dinners en route. The Battalion arrived at SOUES about 5.30 pm Teas on arrival in billets.	
8-7-16. Soues			This day was devoted to interior economy, inspection of feet kit etc. In the afternoon bathing parades were arranged for the men AAA	
9-7-16.			The Battalion formed up in masse, in a field on the HANGEST road, where the C.O delivered an address AAA In the afternoon the officers were addressed by the G.O.C. 21st Division. ~~Write date~~	
10-7-16			At 1.30 am the Battn left billets at SOUES and marched to AILLY-SUR-SOMME, a distance of about 8 miles via PICQUIGNY, arriving there about 5.30 am. Here we entrained for MERICOURT, arriving there at 2 pm by way of AMIENS AAA We were conveyed by motor lorries to MEAULTE AAA Here we bivouaced ~~for~~ until 10.15 pm, when we	

Instructions regarding War Diaries and Intelligence Summaries are contained in F. S. Regs., Part II. and the Staff Manual respectively. Title Pages will be prepared in manuscript.

WAR DIARY
or
INTELLIGENCE SUMMARY
(Erase heading not required.)

Army Form C. 2118.

18

8th (Ser) Batt Leicestershire Regt.

Place	Date	Hour	Summary of Events and Information	Remarks and references to Appendices
	10/7/16.		When the Battalion less 1st Line Transport left for FRICOURT. The 8th Batt went into support of the 7th Batt occupying "Railway Alley" "Sunshine Alley", Willow Trench and "Willow Avenue". One Company remained in reserve in open space behind Willow Trench digging themselves in. Batt HQ situated in Boche dug out in FRICOURT Village	
	10th – 13th		Situation Quiet. Trenches as above were subjected to fairly continuous artillery fire from enemy 120 mm Batteries.	
			The 2nd in Command of Batt & 2nd in Commands of Coys together with 3 NCOs per Coy remained with 1st Line Transport as First reinforcements.	
	13/7/16.		Night of 12/13 Inst the Brigade was relieved, the Coy in support in Railway alley returning to Willow Avenue. Batt HQ & other Coys remaining in same positions. The 6, 7 & 9th Batts returned to the old English line behind FRICOURT.	
	13/7/16	11 am	Conference held at Bde HQ. for all ~~Coy~~ Commanding Officers discussed the arrangements for the attack which was timed to come off on morning of 13th. However the attack was postponed until morning of 14th Inst. Div & Bde Orders for the attack were received on morning of 13 Inst. Coy Commanders went forward to MAMETZ Wood for reconnaissance of ground and jumping off places.	

2449 Wt. W14957/M90 750,000 1/16 J.B.C. & A. Forms/C.2118/12.

Instructions regarding War Diaries and Intelligence Summaries are contained in F. S. Regs., Part II. and the Staff Manual respectively. Title Pages will be prepared in manuscript.

WAR DIARY
or
INTELLIGENCE SUMMARY

(*Erase heading not required.*) 8 (S) Batt Leicestershire Rgt

Army Form C. 2118.

19

Place	Date	Hour	Summary of Events and Information	Remarks and references to Appendices
	13/7/16	3 pm	Another conference at Bde HQ for Commanding Officers. Plan of attack and barrage changed. The 1st East Yorks who were lent to the brigade for purposes of the attack were taken away at the last moment. Owing to the lateness of the hour in receiving these new orders, it was impossible to issue Batt Orders.	
	13/7/16	6 pm	Conference of Coy Commanders etc held at Batt HQ to discuss plan of attack. General plan according to Bde Orders still holds good with the exception that our Artillery barrage on Flat Iron & Forest Trenches lift simultaneously at zero. The attack on the Bazentin-le-Petit Wood to be made by 6th & 7th Batt 6th on right. A Coy of 8th Leic supporting 6th Leic B Coy of 8th Leic supporting 7th Leic. D & C Coys with Batt raiders to be responsible for the left flank of the attack in the place of 1st East Yorks. Every man to carry 2 Mills grenades, 220 rounds SAA, Batt raiders and Platoon Grenade Coys 20 bombs each. 20 picks & 20 shovels were carried by each Coy also green rockets for SOS and green flares for Aeroplane signalling from front line	
	13/7/16	10.30 pm	Batt Raiders, HQ Signallers C & D Coy led by the Commanding Officer & Adjt marched off from behind Welling Trench up the railway track through Mametz	

2449 Wt. W14957/M90 750,000 1/16 J.B.C. & A. Forms/C.2118/12.

Instructions regarding War Diaries and Intelligence Summaries are contained in F. S. Regs., Part II. and the Staff Manual respectively. Title Pages will be prepared in manuscript.

WAR DIARY
or
INTELLIGENCE SUMMARY
(Erase heading not required.) 8th Batt Leicestershire Regt

Army Form C. 2118.

20

Place	Date	Hour	Summary of Events and Information	Remarks and references to Appendices
			Wood to the North edge to take up position for the attack. On the way up C Coy Lewis Gun team knocked out by a shell.	
		2.15 am	The first wave of the attack took up its position in the open 30 yds to North of North edge of Wood, right on Railway track, 7th Leic on left – remaining platoons took up their positions at about 30 yds distances in the Wood. Batt HQ situated in the clearing just off the railway at about X 18 C 6.9 in shell holes.	
			Lines of attack were subjected to heavy bombardment from the enemy during the wait prior to the attack causing a number of casualties.	
			Immediately Batt HQ was established, signallers commenced to run out a line to Bde HQ at X 24 a 3.3. Communication continually broken by enemy Artillery fire.	
		12 midnt	A & B Coys left Willow Trench at about 12 midnight following in rear of 6th Batt round the Eastern side of the Wood, position taken up in hollow in clearing out of observation but subjected to artillery fire.	
	14/7/16	3 am	Dispositions as follows – Batt HQ same place as above – D Coy in 2 lines of 2 platoons with its right on the railway 200 yds in front of N edge of Wood. C Coy moved up to the North edge – B Coy supporting 7th Leic lying in the North East corner of the Wood – A Coy supporting the 6th Leic Regt lying out in the open	

2449 Wt. W14957/M90 750,000 1/16 J.B.C. & A. Forms/C.2118/12.

Instructions regarding War Diaries and Intelligence Summaries are contained in F. S. Regs., Part II. and the Staff Manual respectively. Title Pages will be prepared in manuscript.

WAR DIARY
or
INTELLIGENCE SUMMARY

(Erase heading not required.) 8 (S) Batt Loyal N Lanc Regt

Army Form C. 2118.

21

Place	Date	Hour	Summary of Events and Information	Remarks and references to Appendices
			on the Eastern side of the Wood. Batt raiders & D Coy Bombers were lying out in front of D Coy 1st Wave.	
			During our intense bombardment from 3 am – Enemy subjected the N.E. edge of Wood & the Wood itself to very heavy bombardment and Machine Gun Fire	
		3.25 am	D Coy advanced preceded by the Raiders and Bombers to their objective which was about 100 yds of Villa Trench to the left of railway LOFT Trench & ASTON TRENCH. During intense bombardment they crept up as close as possible. In the actual attack this Coy suffered considerably from hostile Machine Gun Fire, not a single officer of this Coy reaching Villa trench. The Coy was led by its NCOs. Very little opposition was encountered when Villa trench was reached, dug outs were immediately bombed & the Lewis Guns which followed up closely took up a position in Villa trench and caused considerable number of casualties amongst the retreating enemy. Although the majority of the raiders had been knocked out, the remainder did excellent work in bombing outwards towards the left flank & blocking Villa and Aston Trenches. D Coy consolidated their trenches as quickly as possible.	

2449 Wt. W14957/M90 750,000 1/16 J.B.C. & A. Forms/C.2118/12.

Instructions regarding War Diaries and Intelligence Summaries are contained in F. S. Regs., Part II. and the Staff Manual respectively. Title Pages will be prepared in manuscript.

WAR DIARY
or
INTELLIGENCE SUMMARY

(Erase heading not required.) 8th (S) Batt Leicester Regt.

Army Form C. 2118.

22

Place	Date	Hour	Summary of Events and Information	Remarks and references to Appendices
	14/7/16.	4·25 am	At 4·25 am C Coy and 1st Waves of A & B Coys advanced over the 450 yds of No mans land and arrived at Bazentin-le-Petit Wood – C Coy going up the West side of the Wood as far as Forest Trench support eventually advancing with the 7th Batt as far as the North edge of the Wood on the way Bombing the enemy dug outs in the Wood. This Coys final position was from Aston trench to within about 100 yds of North West Corner of Wood. B Coy & A Coy on arrival at the wood pushed forward in support of 7th & 6th Batts the whole then advancing to the North edge of the Wood and Bazentin-le-Petit village. The enemy put up a strong resistance in Forest trench but withdrew to the outskirts of the village and the extreme NE corner of the Wood the time was now about 5 am. During the advance over No mans land a number of casualties ~~were~~ occurred due to enemy Machine guns situated in the middle of the Wood on platforms up large trees.	
		5 am	about 5 am Commanding officer & Adjt. came over to ~~AB~~ SW Corner of Wood where Batt HQ was established.	
		5·25 am	Last Wave of A & B Coys came over & passed right through the Wood	

2449 Wt. W14957/M90 750,000 1/16 J.B.C. & A. Forms/C.2118/12.

Instructions regarding War Diaries and Intelligence Summaries are contained in F. S. Regs., Part II. and the Staff Manual respectively. Title Pages will be prepared in manuscript.

WAR DIARY
or
INTELLIGENCE SUMMARY

(Erase heading not required.) 8th (S) Batt Leicestershire Regt

Army Form C. 2118.

23

Place	Date	Hour	Summary of Events and Information	Remarks and references to Appendices
			to the North edge.	
	14/7/16	5 am	Enemy Counter attacked up Aston & Villa trenches with bombs and rifle grenades. C Coy under 2/Lt Alexander formed bombing parties and drove them back, the latter and the Colonel losing their lives about this time. Their left flank was continually rifle grenaded till about 2.30 pm	
	14/7/16	10 am	Enemy counter attacked the North edge of the Wood but were repulsed by rifle & Lewis Gun fire after 3 hours fighting. About this time 50 men were sent up from Forest Trench where they were consolidating to support C Coy right. Every effort was now made to consolidate positions gained.	
		3 pm	From 3 pm – 4.15 pm enemy bombarded Bazentin le Petit Wood and No Mans Land very heavily, using tear shells. When the 1st East Yorks came up with reinforcements.	
	Night 14/15		North edge of Wood was much troubled by a party of enemy entrenched outside, who caused several casualties with rifle grenades & sniping. This party was eventually driven out by Stokes fire on night of 16/17 Inst.	
	15/7/16	6 am	Batt had orders to ~~[illegible]~~ withdraw to a spot in rear of Mametz Wood together	

2449 Wt. W14957/M90 750,000 1/16 J.B.C. & A. Forms/C.2118/12.

Instructions regarding War Diaries and Intelligence Summaries are contained in F. S. Regs., Part II. and the Staff Manual respectively. Title Pages will be prepared in manuscript.

WAR DIARY
or
INTELLIGENCE SUMMARY
(Erase heading not required.) 8(S) Batt Leicestershire Regt

Army Form C. 2118.

14

Place	Date	Hour	Summary of Events and Information	Remarks and references to Appendices
			with the 7th & 9th Batts. On its arrival it was ordered to resume its position in Bazentin le Petit Wood as soon as possible, which it did. Nothing of importance happened after this till the Battalion was relieved except continual sniping from the enemy.	
			Rations and Water & SAA came up each evening & were successfully distributed except in the case of an isolated party of B Coy in Bazentin Village on evening of 14th.	
	17/7/16	6 am	The Batt was eventually relieved by the DLI on the morning of 17th at about 6 am. The Batt then marched back by Companies to F4b where the transport had been brought up, hot tea was given the men on arrival and Breakfast at about 9 am.	
		6 pm	The Bde moved to Ribemont a distance of about 8 miles via Treux, Denancourt, Fricourt. The Bde was billeted at Ribemont very tightly packed in.	
	18/7/16		Redistribution of Billets, 8 Batt moved to Mericourt during the afternoon & took over new Billets.	
	19/7/16		The Bde paraded in fatigue dress for Inspection of GOC 21st Div, who congratulated the Bde on its magnificent performance in the recent operations	

2449 Wt. W14957/M90 750,000 1/16 J.B.C. & A. Forms/C.2118/12.

Instructions regarding War Diaries and Intelligence Summaries are contained in F. S. Regs., Part II. and the Staff Manual respectively. Title Pages will be prepared in manuscript.

WAR DIARY
or
INTELLIGENCE SUMMARY

Army Form C. 2118.

(Erase heading not required.) 8 (S) Batt Lincoln Regt

25

Place	Date	Hour	Summary of Events and Information	Remarks and references to Appendices
	20/7/16		The Bde received the congratulations of the Div Corps and Army Commanders. Bde moved back into rest billets – the Batt entrained at MERICOURT at 11 am & detrained at SALEUX SW of AMIENS and marched from thence to SOUES (12 miles) arriving there at 7.30 pm. Transport went by road arriving Billets after midnight.	

2449 Wt. W14957/M90 750,000 1/16 J.B.C. & A. Forms/C.2118/12.

Army Form C. 2118.

Instructions regarding War Diaries and Intelligence Summaries are contained in F. S. Regs., Part II. and the Staff Manual respectively. Title Pages will be prepared in manuscript.

WAR DIARY
or
INTELLIGENCE SUMMARY

(Erase heading not required.) 8 Ser Nott Derbyshire Rgt

26

Place	Date	Hour	Summary of Events and Information	Remarks and references to Appendices
			The following Officer, NCOs & men were recommended for immediate reward for acts of gallantry during the operations July 14 – 17th:–	
			Capt H L Beardsley.	
			No 14994 Cpl G W Lings	
			14032 LCpl R W Bennington	
			11473 LCpl R Robinson	
			15460 Pte C W Dale	
			13203 J W Ripley (Pte)	
			11623 Pte W H Toon	
			12171 Pte H Warden	
			10472 Pte A Pitt	
			15699 LCpl G W Black	
			20331 Sergeant S Parsons	
			12708 Sergeant R W Stafford	
			12722 Sergeant S Jeffs.	

2449 Wt. W14957/M90 750,000 1/16 J.B.C. & A. Forms/C.2118/12.

Army Form C. 2118.

Instructions regarding War Diaries and Intelligence Summaries are contained in F. S. Regs., Part II. and the Staff Manual respectively. Title Pages will be prepared in manuscript.

WAR DIARY
or
INTELLIGENCE SUMMARY

(Erase heading not required.) 8 (S.) Batt Cheshire Reg

27

Place	Date	Hour	Summary of Events and Information	Remarks and references to Appendices
			Casualties during Operations July 14th – 17th 1916	

Officer Casualties.

KILLED IN ACTION.
Lt. Col. J. G. Mignon.
2/Lt. A.G.E. Bowell
2/Lt. F.C.G. Greenway
2/Lt. J. Alexander.

DIED OF WOUNDS
2/Lt. J. Lea.

WOUNDED
Capt. F. Ward.
Capt. C.A.B. Elliott
Capt. J. Abbott.
Capt. T.L. Warner.
Lt. N.A.J. Ewen.
2/Lt. V.H.L. Davenport.
2/Lt. E.P. Frake-Walters.
2/Lt. M. Dove
2/Lt. A.E. Gregory
2/Lt. W.S. Murphy
2/Lt. W.G. Jamieson
2/Lt. H.R. Gross.

Casualties of Other Ranks.

KILLED IN ACTION	56
DIED OF WOUNDS	10.
WOUNDED	310
MISSING	39
TOTAL CASUALTIES	415

2449 Wt. W14957/M90 750,000 1/16 J.B.C. & A. Forms/C.2118/12.

Instructions regarding War Diaries and Intelligence Summaries are contained in F. S. Regs., Part II. and the Staff Manual respectively. Title Pages will be prepared in manuscript.

WAR DIARY
or
INTELLIGENCE SUMMARY

(Erase heading not required.) 8th (Ser) Bn Leicestershire Regt

Army Form C. 2118.

28

Place	Date	Hour	Summary of Events and Information	Remarks and references to Appendices
21-7-16 Soues			The morning was spent in kit inspections and Interior Economy AAA In the afternoon we had some bathing parades. We left Soues at 7.20 pm and marched to the cross. roads, where we halted for about 2 hours, when we were met by motor buses, which conveyed us to LONGPRÉ, arriving there about 11 pm AAA Here we bivouacked for the night	
22-7-16 Longpré			We left here at 1 pm and marched to LONGUEAU via the outskirts of AMIENS, arriving there about 3.30 pm. Here we entrained at 4.15 pm for ST. POL arriving there about 10.30 pm. We bivouacked for the night in a field about 1½ miles outside the town	
23-7.16			We left here at 10 am and marched to GOUY-EN-TERNOIS a distance of about 10 ~~kilometres~~, arriving there about 12.30 pm AAA We billeted here for the night. ~~and~~	
24-7.16 Gouy-en-Ternois			We left here about 5.30 pm and were conveyed by motor-bus to LATTRE-ST-QUENTIN, arriving there about 7.30 pm, and proceeded to billets.	
25-7-16 Lattre St. Quentin			This day was allotted to Interior Economy, particular attention being paid to gas helmets.	
26-7-16 Lattre St. Quentin			The CO and Company Commanders proceeded by bus to visit the trenches, ~~AAA~~ we were going to take over AAA Company parades were carried on as usual. Specialists under their various instructors.	

2449 Wt. W14957/M90 750,000 1/16 J.B.C. & A. Forms/C.2118/12.

Army Form C. 2118.

25

Instructions regarding War Diaries and Intelligence Summaries are contained in F. S. Regs., Part II. and the Staff Manual respectively. Title Pages will be prepared in manuscript.

WAR DIARY
or
INTELLIGENCE SUMMARY

(Erase heading not required.)

8th (Ser) Bn Leicestershire Regt

Place	Date	Hour	Summary of Events and Information	Remarks and references to Appendices
Lattre St. Quentin	27-7-16.		The morning was devoted to Interior Economy AAA We left here at 2pm, marching to WANQUETIN, where we bivouaced until 7.30pm, when we continued our march to ARRAS, arriving there about 10.30pm AAA The Battalion were billeted in the barracks, and the officers in billets in the town. The Lewis Gun Officer and men went straight forward to the trenches, and took over from the 6th D.C.L.I.	
Arras	28-7-16		The Battalion took over the trenches held by the 6th D.C.L.I. which comprised Trenches 98–101 inclusive. The Battalion on our right was the 9th Leicesters and the Battalion on our left the Rifle Brigade. Details for relief and Operation Orders enclosed. D Coy took over Sector (98–99) on the right, and C Coy (100–101) on the left, A+B Coys going into Support.	
Trenches 98-101	29-7-16		On the night of the 28/29 a large fleet of aeroplanes passed over on their way to the enemy's lines AAA The enemy succeeded in getting one of these alight, and it came to earth turning a somersaults sideways AAA It appeared impossible for the occupants to escape, and it was much to our surprise that we learnt later the occupants were practically unhurt AAA The night passed off very quietly.	
Trenches (98-101)	30-7-16		During the ~~night~~ early part of the night of the 28th the enemy fired some Rifle grenades into the right of our sector (98) AAA No damage was done AAA During the night sent up an exceptional number of Very Lights AAA We had a wiring-party in front of 99 Sector.	

2449 Wt. W14957/M90 750,000 1/16 J.B.C. & A. Forms/C.2118/12.

Army Form C. 2118.

WAR DIARY
or
INTELLIGENCE SUMMARY

(Erase heading not required.) 8th (Serv) Bn Leicestershire Regt.

30

Instructions regarding War Diaries and Intelligence Summaries are contained in F. S. Regs., Part II. and the Staff Manual respectively. Title Pages will be prepared in manuscript.

Place	Date	Hour	Summary of Events and Information	Remarks and references to Appendices
31-7-16. Trenches (98-101)			The enemy's artillery were very active between 12.30pm and 1.45pm AAA The shells chiefly were 5.9". Their objective apparently was "Claude" Crater. AAA Some shells also fell in our Support Trenches, but without doing any damage. We continued work on dug-outs etc, and deepening NOVEMBER AVENUE AAA	
			[signature] Major Comndg 8 Leic Regt. 31/7/16	

2449 Wt. W14957/M90 750,000 1/16 J.B.C. & A. Forms/C.2118/12.

A P P E N D I C E S .

SECRET

Copy No 8

110th Brigade Operation Order No 28

Ref - Hectograph map issued herewith.

July 13th 1916.

I An attack will be carried out at ZERO on the 14th July, as stated in 21st Div. OO No 59 dated 11/7/16, issued to all units.

II The 110th Inf Bde will capture and consolidate BAZENTIN-LE-PETIT WOOD and that part of the village of BAZENTIN-LE-PETIT lying to the West of the BAZENTIN-LE-PETIT to MARTINPUICH Road (exclusive)

Connection with the III Corps on the north will be established at S. 7. d 3. 1.

III The 1st East Yorks Regt are placed at the disposal of the 110th Bde for the purpose of this attack, and will protect the left flank.

IV Positions of, and times for forming up at positions of assembly will be notified later.

V Maps showing positions of barrages and strong points to be consolidated have been issued to all concerned.

VI Barrages will lift at the following hours:-

0 + 60 minutes
0 + 95 "
0 + 120 "
0 + 140 "
0 + 160 "
0 + 190 "

The attacking waves must follow close on the barrage when it lifts.

VII The 110th Inf. Bde will attack in six waves, as follows, the 6th Bn Leic Regt being on the right and the 7th Bn Leic Regt on the left:-

'A' wave - 16 platoons of the 6th Bn Leic Regt and 16 platoons of the 7th Bn Leic Regt in three lines of column of platoons at 30 yards distance.

'B' wave 4 platoons of the 6th Bn Leic Regt and 4 platoons of the 7th Bn Leic Regt in line.

'C' wave 4 platoons of the 8th Bn Leic Regt in line, 2 platoons being in support of the 6th Bn and 2 platoons in support of the 7th Bn.

'D' wave as in 'C' wave

'E' wave as in 'C' wave

'F' wave as in 'C' wave, but all men carrying

Each wave will be self contained, carrying its own bombs etc.

VIII The left of the 7th Bn Leic Regt will rest on the tram line running from X.18.a.9.3 to S.7.d.3.1 and thence on the western edge of BAZENTIN-LE-PETIT wood: the right of the 7th Bn will rest on the junction of road and MAMETZ Wood at S.13.d.6½.9 (exclusive) thence to where road crosses enemy wire at S.14.a.1½.6½, thence to clearing in BAZENTIN-LE-PETIT Wood at S.8.c.3½.6. following the line of clearing to S.8.a.6.7.

The left of the 6th Bn will rest on the right of the 7th Bn Leic Regt as far as the Southern edge of clearing running from S.8.c.3½.6. to S.8.c.9.4½; the right of the 6th Bn Leic Regt will be on the road running from the eastern corner of MAMETZ Wood, S.20.a.1.8 to road junction S.14.b.1.5, to road along east edge of BAZENTIN-LE-PETIT Wood to MARTINPUICH (these roads exclusive).

IX. The 6th Bn Leicesters on reaching the clearing in BAZENTIN-LE-PETIT wood will not cross it until the VIIth Division and themselves have made good the buildings on their right flank.

X. At 0 (ZERO) 'A' wave will enter the enemy front line trench, the leading line of platoons proceeding on to the S. edge of BAZENTIN-LE-PETIT wood, the remaining two lines consolidating the enemy trench.

A

At 0+60 'B' wave will join the two first lines of 'A' wave, the whole proceeding into FOREST TRENCH, the 3rd line of 'A' wave remaining in the enemy first line trench to complete consolidation.

At 0+95 'C' wave will enter enemy first line trench, and continue to consolidate it – the whole of 'A' and 'B' waves will take up a line along the road running East to West in BAZENTIN-LE-PETIT wood, from S.8.d.1½.3 to S.7.d.5.7½.

At 0+120 'D' wave will enter FOREST TRENCH, and 'A' & 'B' take up a line from S.7.d.6.9 to junction of six roads at S.8.c.½.8½ inclusive, along south side of clearing to BAZENTIN-LE-PETIT to MARTIN PUICH road.

At 0+140 'E' wave will occupy line occupied by 'A' and 'B' at 0+120.
'A' and 'B' waves will take up a line running from NW corner of BAZENTIN-LE-PETIT wood to clearing about S.8.a.4.7.

At 0+160 'F' wave will proceed to line occupied by 'E' wave, where they will deposit their loads and form a support.
'A' and 'B' waves will occupy a line from N.E. corner of BAZENTIN wood to road junction at S.8.c.9½.7.

At 0+190 A and B waves will occupy their final objective.

XI At 0+190 when final objective is occupied units will be disposed as follows:–

(a) 7th Bn Leic Regt:– from NW corner of BAZENTIN-LE-PETIT wood at S. 7. b. 7 4. along the northern edge of wood, along hedge to MARTIN PUICH road at S. 8. a. 8. 6½.

The 7th Bn will occupy Strong points numbers 10, 11 and 13.

(b) The 6th Bn Leic Regt. all that part of village West of MARTIN PUICH road (exclusive) except hedge on northern extremity of village, for which 7th Bn is responsible.

The 6th Bn will occupy Strong Points numbers 7, 8 and 9.

(c) 8th Bn Leic Regt: Strong Points. 1, 2, 4 and 5.

Men not employed in consolidating will be collected at convenient supporting centres.

XII The 1st Bn. E Yorks Regt will be responsible for the left flank of the attack.

At ZERO two platoons will enter enemy first line trench & 2 platns enemy 2nd line Trench and form Blocks in LEFT ALLEY, and NW of the junction of LEFT ALLEY and VILLA TRENCH & Aston Trench. Two platoons will enter with each successive wave and will work up the west side of BAZENTIN-LE-PETIT wood, keeping in touch with the leading wave.

The East Yorks will be responsible for LEFT ALLEY.

They will move from MAMETZ WOOD on the West side of the tramway, their right keeping touch with the left of each successive wave.

When the final objective is occupied, they will be disposed as follows:—

On West side of BAZENTIN WOOD to the NW corner at S.7.b.7.4.

Strong Points 3, 6, 12

~~1 Coy in Reserve in MAMETZ WOOD.~~

XIII The 9th Bn Leic Regt will be in Reserve in MAMETZ WOOD. Their exact position will will be notified later.

XIV The 110th Machine Gun Coy will cover the left flank of the attack and will send forward 2 guns to the north end of BAZENTIN-LE-PETIT wood. ~~Separate orders attached~~.

XV One Stokes Mortar will accompany the 6th & 7th Bns Leic Regt.

Two spare mortars will be kept in MAMETZ WOOD. Mortars will cross No mans land with "B" wave.

XVI Special instructions will be given to the O.C. FLAMMENWERFER.

XVII Two dumps will be formed at the northern end of MAMETZ WOOD. Location will be notified later. The R.E. are cutting paths to these dumps. Each dump will contain

300 Stokes Mortar Bombs
5000 bombs
250 Rifle grenades
20000 Rounds S.A.A.

Empty bomb buckets must be returned to these dumps at every opportunity.

Full boxes of ammunition will not be carried by carriers, they will take up ten bandoliers.

A large dump will be established at X.24.a.2.3.

XVIII 220 rounds per rifle will be carried on the man, also two bombs and two sandbags.

A percentage of picks and shovels will be carried.

Water bottles must be filled.

XIX Rations for the 14th inst will be issued on the morning of the 13th inst.

XX Each Bn will furnish a total of six runners to Bde HQ. These will report to the Brigade signalling officer at 6 pm 13th inst.

XXI An advance report centre will be established in MAMETZ WOOD, location will be notified later.

XXII Watches will be synchronised at Bde HQ at 6 pm 13th inst. One officer from each unit will attend for this purpose.

XXIII Attention is called to 21st Div G 52 of 12th inst. OC 110th MG Coy and 110th TM Bty can see this at Bde HQ

XXIV Bde HQ will close at FRICOURT at 10.30p and reopen at 11.30 pm at X.24.a.3.2

Issued at 9.15 pm

Copy No 1 – 21st Div.
2 – 62nd Bde
3 – 64th Bde
4 – 1st Bde
5 – Bde
6 – 6th Leicester Regt
7 – 7th
8 – 8th
9 – 9th
10 – 110 MG Coy
11 – 110 TM Bty
12 – 1st E Yorks Regt
13 – Office

A W Stricker Major
Bde Major
110 Inf Bde

21st Div G 50

110th Inf Bde

Until Zero on the day of attack, Brigades are responsible for moving bombs, rifle grenades, Stokes Mortar ammunition, forward from ROSE COTTAGE.

After Zero, the Division will be responsible for moving these stores and any R.E. Stores required, from ROSE COTTAGE dump to the bend in WILLOW AVENUE at X 29 b 5.6 where an intermediate dump is being made.

The 64th Bde will detail 3 complete platoons to report to Lieut Maughan (Asst. Div. Grenadier Officer) at ROSE COTTAGE dump (road junction F 4 c 5.6) one hour before zero. This party will revert to their Bde and will rejoin their Bn three hours after Zero.

Stragglers which have been collected by the A.P.M will be used for carrying as soon as they arrive at ROSE COTTAGE.

Bdes. will communicate their requirements to Lieut. Maughan through H.Q at FRICOURT CHATEAU

Bdes will still be responsible for movement of stores forward from dump at F 4 c 5.6 after Zero.

sd H E Franklin Major
General Staff, 21st Div

6th Bn Leicesters
7th
8th
9
110 M.G. Coy

For information

A W Fletcher Major
Brigade Major
110th Inf. Bde

12/7/16.

21 Div. O.O. No. 60.

[redacted] 17

13th July, 1916. 15

Reference 21 Div. O.O. 59 dated 11.7.16.

1. The attack will take place at 3.25 a.m. on 14th July.

2. The bombardment will be continued at the normal rate throughout the night of July 13/14th. There will be an intense bombardment from 3.20 a.m. to 3.25 a.m. on July 14th. At 3.25 a.m. the bombardment will lift as shown on maps issued herewith.

3. Green flares for indicating the position of front line to aeroplanes will be used. 300 of these are being issued to the 110th Bde. and 200 to the 64th Bde.

4. The O.C. Div'l Signal Coy. will arrange to synchronise time with units between 6 p.m. and 7 p.m. on July 13th.

5. The maps issued herewith show the successive lifts of Artillery after Zero on July 14th. Maps already issued showing these lifts are inaccurate and are to be destroyed.

6. All troops of the 21st Division moving up to the line will be clear of the cross-roads F 7 c by 10.30 p.m. on July 13th.

7. The 1st Division is occupying CONTALMAISON VILLA during the night of 13/14th July, and will demonstrate with fire on the trench running N.W. from S 7 d 3.1, care being taken not to fire into BAZENTIN - LE - PETIT WOOD during our advance through the wood. The 1st Division is also arranging to connect Point S 7 d 3.1 to LOWER WOOD by means of troops lying out with Lewis Guns.

8. The note to para (6) of the above quoted O.O. is cancelled

9. MIDDLE ALLEY running from MAMETZ WOOD to enemy's Second Line will be used only for "UP" traffic until the second objective has been captured, after which hour it will be used for "DOWN" traffic only. Picquets will be found by 110th Bde. to ensure that this order is carried out.

10. Acknowledge.

H L Gamblyn Major
for. Lieut.Colon
G.S. 21 Di

Issued at 6 a.m. to -

	copy No.		Copy No.
War Diary & File	1 - 2	Signals.	26
XV Corps	3	"Q"	28 - 30
62 Inf. Bde.	4 - 8	A.D.M.S.	31
64 " "	9 - 13	A.P.M.	32
110 " "	14 - 18	C.Comdt.	33
Div. Art.	19 - 20	D.A.D.O.S.	34
Div. Eng.	21 - 24	1st Div.	35
[illegible]	25	7th Div.	36

7. Stokes Mortars will be used on the same principle as Artillery Batteries - moving by bounds from one suitable position to another, and NOT moving blindly on with the advancing Infantry.

8. Men detailed specially for carrying up grenades will only carry 50 rounds of S.A.A.
A load for a carrier will be 2 buckets with 18 grenades in each.
Carriers going forward with the attack will carry two buckets each with 10 grenades in it.

9. A proportion of N.C.O's will each carry a packet of cartridges for rifle grenades in his pockets.

10. The A.P.M. will arrange for a "flying patrol" to collect stragglers in FRICOURT Village.

11. German prisoners will be handed over to the A.P.M. at ROSE COTTAGE, and forwarded thence, under Divisional arrangements, to the Cage at MEAULTE.
Escorts will be reduced to a minimum.

12. On completion of carrying duty, stragglers will be marched to the nearest Bde. H.Q. whence they will be forwarded to their own Bde. H.Q. or units when it is convenient to do so.

13. Water is laid on to ~~ROSE~~ RED COTTAGE. ~~Pails or~~ Petrol tins for carrying and storing water have been issued to Bdes.
Water carts will be sent up at night with rations, wagons and if required they will be sent up by day to any point selected by ~~C.O's and Bdes.~~ Bde. Comdrs.
There is a well and pump at X 22 c 6.1. The pump is now being repaired.

14. Rations will be sent up to any place appointed by ~~C.O's and Bdes.~~ Bde. Comdrs. If no other instructions are received they will be sent to ROSE COTTAGE at 9 p.m. where they should be met by guides.

15. The tramway from ROSE COTTAGE to BOTTOM WOOD can be used for rations, ammunition etc. This tramway will be joined up as soon as possible at X 29 b 3.6 with the line running through MAMETZ WOOD.

16. An Advanced Dressing Station will be established in FRICOURT.
When the situation permits a Collecting Station will be established at X 29 b 5.6.
Walking cases will be directed to the Subway F 7 b 5.5.

H. W. Gaulbyn. Major
for Lieut-Colonel,
General Staff,
21st Division.

12/7/16.

SECRET.

21 Div.
G.70.

110 Inf. Bde.	5	copies
62 : :	1	:
64 : :	1	:
Div. Art.	1	:
Div. Eng.	1	:
Signals	1	:
Pioneers	1	:

The following extracts from 7th Division O.O.81 dated 12th July 1916, are forwarded for information:-

OBJECTIVES.

(a) The attack will be delivered with the 20th Infantry Brigade in the front followed by the 22nd Infantry Brigade, with the 91st Infantry Brigade in reserve.

(b) Objectives of the 20th Infantry Brigade.

1st Objective.
The enemy's front line trenches between point S 15 c 15.40 and the Road at S 14 a 70.35.

2nd Objective.
The enemy's support line from point S 15 a 25.10 to the point in BAZENTIN-LE-GRAND WOOD where CIRCUS Trench turns Northwards, thence straight to the Western edge of the WOOD.

3rd Objective.
The whole of BAZENTIN-LE-GRAND WOOD.
The 20th Infantry Brigade will not advance beyond their third objective.

(c) Objectives of the 22nd Infantry Brigade.

To capture BAZENTIN-LE-PETIT Village East of the MARTINPUICH Road (road inclusive) and the CEMETERY, and to establish a line from S 15 a 20.95 (where a junction will be made with XIII Corps) through the CEMETERY to the Northern exit of BAZENTIN-LE-PETIT Village where a junction will be made with the 21st Division. The 22nd Infantry Brigade will be prepared to attack the houses West of the MARTINPUICH Road should the 21st Division be delayed.
Advances will be timed in accordance with the times shewn on the barrage map attached, the infantry moving as close up to the forward line of the barrage as possible just before the time when the fire will lift.

CONSOLIDATION.

(a) Each objective or line gained will be consolidated at once.

P.T.O.

(b) Strong Points will be established at:-

(1) S 14 b 2.3.
(2) S 14 b 65.50.
(3) S 15 a 25.90.
(4) A Machine Gun position in the WOOD at S 15 a 10.85 to cover the cross-roads.
(5) A "Keep" consisting of a group of houses surrounding point S 8 d 2.7; arrangements being made to fire up the MARTINPUICH Road.
(6) Northern corner of WOOD covering CEMETERY S 8 b 9.1.
(7) The North end of the BAZENTIN-LE-PETIT Village will be prepared for all round defence.

ASSEMBLY OF TROOPS.

The following positions are placed at the disposal of Brigadiers for the assembly of their Brigades:-

To the 20th Infantry Brigade -
CATERPILLAR WOOD and the trenches East of a line from the Western end of CATERPILLAR WOOD to BLACK ALLEY with the exception of WHITE Trench.

To the 22nd Infantry Brigade -
The portion of MAMETZ WOOD within the Divisional area. WHITE Trench, CLIFF Trench and FRITZ Trench.

HEADQUARTERS.

20th Infantry Brigade - POMMIERS REDOUBT.

22nd Infantry Brigade - WHITE Trench at point S 25 b 8.6.

[signature]

Lieut-Colonel,

General Staff,
21st Division.

13/7/16.

S E C R E T .

21 Div.
G.52.

62nd Inf. Bde.	5
64th : :	5
110th : :	5
Div. Art.	2
Div. Eng.	4
Pioneers	1
Signals	1
"Q"	3
A.P.M.	1
A.D.M.S.	1
Capt. Franklin,	1
Lieut. Maughan,	1

Reference 21 Div. O.O.59 dated 11/7/16.

1. Not more than 25 Officers per Battalion will go into action. If Battalions have less than 35 Officers, the number going into action will be proportionately reduced.
This order refers to all three Brigades.
50% of officers left behind will be collected in the vicinity of cross roads F 9 a 5.7, and will come under the command of the senior officer present, who will not rejoin his Battalion until all officers have gone forward. The senior officer will arrange for these officers to march stragglers, as directed in following order.
The remainder of the officers left behind will remain with the 1st Line Transport.

2. Stragglers will be collected at cross roads F 9 a 5.7, where they will be given a meal.
As soon as a sufficient party has been collected, it will be marched by an Officer to ROSE COTTAGE Dump, where the officer will receive orders from Lieut. Maughan, Divisional Stokes Mortar Officer.
Each Brigade will detail one particularly efficient N.C.O. to take charge of stragglers on arrival at the cross roads.

3. 110th Inf. Bde. will be responsible for picquet ing communication trenches between the new German front line and support trench, and MIDDLE AVENUE.
62nd Inf. Bde. will make its own arrangements for picquet ing MAMETZ WOOD.
64th Inf. Bde. will picquet QUADRANGLE ALLEY, WOOD TRENCH, BOTTOM ALLEY and the Valley East of BOTTOM WOOD.

4. C.R.E. will arrange to improve MIDDLE ALLEY as soon as it is convenient to do so.

5. The Pioneers will be placed under the orders of the C.R.E. until further orders.

6. Battalion Signals will not follow closely in rear of Battalion H.Q. during a forward move, but will wait until a route has been reconnoitred . Until a Bn. H.Q. and its Signals have joined up, communication will be carried out from the new to the old position by runner.

S E C R E T.

21 Div.
G.90.

XV Corps	1
62nd Inf. Bde.	5
64th : :	5
110th : :	5
Div. Art.	2
Div. Eng.	4
Pioneers	1
Signals	1
"Q"	3
A.D.M.S.	1
A.P.M.	1
C.Comdt.	1
D.A.D.O.S.	1
1st Div.	1
7th Div.	1

Reference 21 Div. O.O.59 dated 11/7/16.

AMENDMENT.
Para 3.

1st Objective for 21st Division should read :-

" To capture enemy defences (front and support trenches) between the line of the road running from East corner of MAMETZ WOOD S 20 a 1.8 through Pt. S 14 b 0775 to BAZENTIN-LE-PETIT and West edge of BAZENTIN-LE-PETIT WOOD (see LONGUEVAL 1/10,000 Map and attached tracing No.1.)"

INFORMATION REGARDING THE ENEMY.

Identifications obtained from prisoners shows conclusively that the enemy appears to be very disorganized.

We have captured prisoners belonging to reserves normally stationed along the front from CHAMPAGNE to YPRES.

Many of the prisoners have owned to the fact that they have been hurried up ~~from~~ to the front line and have had little or no idea of where they were going to and what they were to do.

There seems little doubt that the German heavy guns have been withdrawn to positions further in rear, but we must expect to meet a considerable number of machine guns, though it is hardly probable that the emplacements will be so strong as those which we have met with in the front line system.

Orders were issued by the G.O.C. 28th Reserve Division "With reference to the improvement of positions". The orders appear to have been very hurriedly written and not at all in the usual precise methods of the German General Staff.

Our heavy/and Field Artillery have been very successful with their fire on the German 2nd Line during the last two days. We may, therefore, confidently assume that the enemy are not in the same fighting form as they were on the 26th June and will probably not fight so well as they did on the 1st July.

for AllSparks ?? RE
Lieut-Colonel,
General Staff,
21st Division.

13/7/16.

S E C R E T.

21 Div.
G.59.

XV Corps	1
62nd Inf. Bde.	5
64th : :	5
110th : :	5
Div. Art.	2
Div. Eng.	4
Pioneers	1
Signals	1
"Q"	3
A.D.M.S.	1
A.P.M.	1
C.Comdt.	1
D.A.D.O.S.	1
1st Div.	1
7th Div.	1

---

1. The Battalion of the 64th Bde. attached to 110th Bde. (vide para 7, 21 Div. O.O.59) will not be used by the Brigadier 110th Bde. for the defence of his left unless he finds it absolutely necessary to do so. It is advisable to endeavour to make good the defence of the BAZENTIN-LE-PETIT WOOD and Village (as directed in 21 Div. O.O.59) with the 110th Bde., so that 64th Bde. can be kept intact as a Divisional Reserve as long as possible.

2. 64th Bde. (less Battalion under orders of 110th Bde.) will remain in positions, which Battalions occupy tonight, and will receive orders to move direct from Div. H.Q.

3. 1st Line Transport will be parked at the West end of MEAULTE.

A L Sparks ?? Maj.
for Lieut-Colonel,
General Staff,
21st Division.

13/7/16.

Copy No. 15

21 Div. O.O. No. 61.

18th July 1916.

Ref:- MARTINPUICH Map. 1/20,000

1. (a) The 4th Army will continue the attack on 19th July in conjunction with the Reserve Army and French 6th Army at an hour Zero.

(b) The XV Corps is to attack HIGH WOOD and the German SWITCH Line between HIGH WOOD and the RAILWAY Line at S 2 a 0.2.

2. The position, when gained, is at once to be consolidated. A Support Line will be dug behind SWITCH TRENCH at the earliest opportunity.

3. The 21st Division will be in Corps Reserve and will be ready to move at 2 hours notice from Zero on 19th July.

4. Today, and on any following days during which the Division is in Reserve, every effort will be made to re-organise Lewis Gun Detachments by training fresh Officers and men.

Grenadier Squads will be reorganised as far as possible, and the number of bombs carried by each Battalion should be made up. Demands for bombs and buckets should be made to 21st Division "Q" as soon as possible.

176
900

5. Brigades, R.E.Companies and Pioneers will forward to Div. H.Q. tomorrow morning table showing strength in Officers and O.R. per unit fit to return to action.

15, 450
17, 560

This table will only show numbers of Officers and O.R. who would move forward in an attack and will not include 1st Line

P.T.O.

Transport and others who would normally be left behind.

6. Div. H.Q. will remain in their present position.

A Paley Lieut-Colonel,
General Staff,
21st Division.

Issued at 10.0 a.m. to

	Copy No.
War Diary & File	1 - 2
62nd Inf. Bde.	3 - 7
64th : :	8 - 12
110th : :	13 - 17
Div. Eng.	18 - 21
Pioneers	22
Signals	23
"Q"	24 - 26
A.D.M.S.	27
A.P.M.	28
C.Comdt.	29
D.A.D.O.S.	30

A Translation of a German Operation Order captured on the evening of the 11th inst. in CONTALMAISON. The order was issued by the 28th Res. Division on the 4th instant.

DIVISIONAL ORDERS WITH REFERENCE TO IMPROVEMENT OF POSITIONS.

---

1. Work on the front line, of a durable nature, is to be undertake if this has not already been done.
Every possible means and effort are to be used to complete this

2. The construction of a second line of trenches behind the first line is to be carried out immediately with all the resources at our disposal. In the Sector held by the 190th Regt. this line will be that which connects OVILLERS and CONTALMAISON. In the Sector held by the 163rd Regt. the second line referred to will begin from CONTALMAISON and will run through the middle of MAMETZ WOOD and afterwards in an easterly and then in a northerly direction and will join the second line West of the road MAMETZ - BAZENTIN-le-PETIT.
Particularly important is the construction of a second trench in the 20th B.I.Bde. sector. This must be so constructed that it lie on the reverse slope to that of the enemy. In so far as the present trenches will not permit the accommodation of supports, the supports must be quartered in existing suitable points where the banking etc. will permit of the quick construction of dug-outs. In the same way, the many dug-outs which still remain undamaged must be used not only for quartering troops, but also for constructing strong points with. The defence of the sectors held by the troops is assured, even when as a result of enemy shell fire the holding of a continuous line is rendered impossible at certain points. The obstacle formed by the dug-outs grouped together in strong points, will prevent the enemy from breaking through, especially if flank fire support is assured from these groups of dug-outs.

3. Of particular importance for the defence is the quick building in of machine-guns behind the front defence line, which command the ground behind and which, with flank fire can support each other, so that enemy forces which may at any point have temporarily broken through, may be held up by machine-gun fire from further advance.

4. Furthermore, behind the front line the conversion of villages into strong points (see para 2) is of greatest importance.
Such villages are :-
POZIERES CONTALMAISON
BAZENTIN-LE-PETIT
BAZENTIN-LE-GRAND and
LONGUEVAL.

5. The strong points of defence which exist in the West, South and East edges of POZIERES must be put into a state of defence at once, so that the possession of this village is assured under all circumstances

6. The gap between the second and third positions North of the line LONGUEVAL - BAZENTIN must be closed with a cross line of trenches, which will commence at about the cross-roads (Three trees) running to BAZENTIN-LE-PETIT, POZIERES, CONTALMAISON - MARTINPUICH. It will join the third line South of FLERS via Hill 154 S.E. of MARTINPUICH and Hill 155 (S.4.d.28) E. of FOUREAUX WOOD (HIGH WOOD). The commencement of this work is to be put in hand at once by the Pioneer Commander.

(Sgd) V.HAHN.

XV CORPS SUMMARY OF INFORMATION.

Information regarding enemy.

A summary of identifications is attached.

In addition to the 7 officers and 647 men captured yesterday was one officer the commander of the LEHR Regiment, a Lt. Col. He stated his regiment had suffered heavily owing to being without proper cover under heavy artillery fire.

According to a document dated 11th July 1916, the 2nd Battn of the 184th Regt was placed under the orders of the 3rd Guard Division and attached to the LEHR Regt.

Prisoners' Statements.

A man of the 1st Battery, 44th Foot Artillery Battalion stated that he arrived from the neighbourhood of LORETTO about the 30th. June and was attached to the 28th Reserve Division.

A prisoner of the 5th Guard Field Artillery Regiment stated that they were expecting heavy artillery to their aid. He stated that the 185th Heavy Battery, 21 c.m. mortars, arrived 2 days ago.

A prisoner of the 26th Infantry Regiment states he was relieved near LORETTO 5 days ago by 162nd Regt.

IDENTIFICATIONS ON XV CORPS FRONT.

55th Landwehr Brigade Ersatz Battn. Prisoner joind Battn 5 days ago with a draft of 28 men from 40th L.W.R. 28th L.W. Division in the VOSGES. Battalion had suffered heavily and only 130 rifles per Company after getting draft. For two days worked on SWITCH line in HIGH WOOD; 1.80 metres deep and no wire where he has been working. 55th were resting at LASSINCOURT 25 kilometres back where he saw no other units. This unit was formerly attached to 52nd Division.

9th Grenadier Regt. (3rd Guard Division) 3 days ago 9th Grenadier Regt were relieved by 165th Regt. and went back to near BAPAUME where they rested for 2 days. They received no drafts. They had previously lost 2/3rds. of their strength and were put into the fight as a Composite Battalion, i.e. 3 Battalions formed into one. Saw 122nd I.R. and 190th I.R. refitting.

190th Regiment, 185th Division. 1st Battalion.
The 190th I.R. went back to VELU for 4 days, 8 - 12th July. At VELU they received drafts of new men. Prisoners Coy received 60 men but they only went into fight with 120 rifles. Draft all young men from Germany.
Men of the 2nd and 3rd Battalions were captured in BAZENTIN LE PETIT WOOD on the 14th.

XV Corps (I).
15th July 1916.

8th Leicester

UNITS IDENTIFIED BY PRISONERS TAKEN DURING
ADVANCE ON GERMAN SECOND LINE.

-:-:-:-:-:-:-:-:-:-:-:-

3rd Guard Division.

Regiment	Bn.	Date 14	Date 15
Lehr	2	44	2
	3	3	5
274 Pioneer Coy.	-	1	
Guard Fusilier (Recruit Co)	1	25	2
3rd Sanitary Co.	-	3	
5th Guard Res. F.A.R.	-	1	2

185th Division.

Regiment	Bn.	14	15
190th	1		73
	2	6	14
	3	54	4
185th	2	6	
185th Pioneer Co.	-	1	
39th Sanitary Co.	-	18	

183rd Division.

Regiment	Bn.	14	15
184th	1	2	
	2	40	8
	3	3	3
9th M.Gun S.Section	-	1	
38th Sanitary Co.	-	1	
183rd F.A.R.	-	2	

10th Bavarian Division.

Regiment	Bn.	14	15
16th Bavarian	1	-	11
	2	-	-
	3	204	37
37th M.G.S.S.	-	-	1

2nd Guard Reserve Division.

Regiment	Bn.	14	15
91st Reserve	1	227	
106th M.G.S.S.	-	1	

7th Division.

Regiment	Bn.	14	15
165th	3	-	4
26th	1	-	14
	2	-	1
	3	-	56

P.T.O.

Also men or officers of the following units:-

Musketen Battalion 117th Regt. 25th Div.	5 men.
1st Battery of Foot Artillery Battalion 44 attached to 28th Reserve Division.	1 Officer & 2 men.
8th Battery of 12th Reserve Field Artillery Regiment.	2 men.

The above is correct to 9 a.m. on 15th July, 1916.

EXAMINATION OF PRISONERS.

Richard Matthes, 4th. Coy. 1st Bn. 91st R.Regt, 2nd Guard Res.Div. Captured West of MAMETZ WOOD early on morning of 13th. July.

They relieved part of the 184th Regt. on the evening of the 11th.

The 119th R.I.R. was supposed to be on their right.

The 2 other battalions of their regiment were somewhere North of them, in reserve.

He states that he has seen men of the following units:-

15th. R.I.R.
77th R.I.R.
119th R.I.R.
Infantry marked 57.
Artillery marked 207.

The roads are in good condition round about BAPAUME.
Prisoner was not very bright.

Two prisoners of the 1st Coy. 28th Pioneer Battn., belonging to the 3rd Guard Divn. were captured.
They confirm that 274 Field Coy. was also attached.
3 Zuge (180) were acting as infantry in MAMETZ WOOD and the remainder of them (60) were digging behind BAZENTIN LE PETIT.

Prisoner of 2nd Battn. Lehr Regiment, 3rd Guard Division.

Captured in MAMETZ WOOD.

Two prisoners state they have seen men of the 223rd R.I.R. in MAMETZ WOOD yesterday (?).

A prisoner of the 184th I.R. stated that the 9th Machine Gun Marksman Section is attached to the 183rd Division.
Also confirms that 38th Landwehr Sanitary Coy. is attached.

Prisoners captured today by the XV Corps as follows:-

	Offrs.	O.R.
38 Sanitaet Co.		1
1st Coy. 28th Pioneer Co.		2
184th. Regt. 1st Bn.		1
Total		4
In field ambulances ..		20
Total		24
Total to date captured by XV Corps	65	3,804

XV Corps.

13th July 1916.

Capt Weatherill

A 2 Lt Oliver
2 Lt Child

B Capt Beardsley
Lt Harris

Major McCutcheon
C Lt Bennet
2 Lt Reeves

D Lt Goodliffe
Lt Goodacre

Sig officer

Outstanding. Lt Harris to B.
Lt Goodliffe to Comd D

EXAMINATION OF PRISONER MAX BORUS, SANITAETSOLDAT,
Captured on morning 12th July in MAMETZ WOOD.

=

Prisoner states there is a trench rumour that 2 Army Corps are coming up to support them - one from Russia and one a Bavarian Corps.

Prisoner describes German losses as very heavy - 4 divisions being practically out of action. Prisoner named 183rd, 185th and 3rd Guard Divisions, and says 190th I.R. suffered especially heavily. Of many companies only 15 to 20 men could be collected.

Prisoner describes confusion behind German line as very bad. He states a number of men from various Coys. and Regts. would be collected from stragglers in rear and pushed into the fight. He says he has heard that many officers had been shot by their own men.

He met men of a division from VERDUN (?) who considered this fight very much worse than anything they had experienced down there.

Prisoners' company lost 2 men killed 7 men and 3 horses wounded from our artillery fire before his Sanitats Company reached BAZENTIN.

XV Corps (I).
13th. July 1916.

8th Leic Rgt

8th Leicesters

PRISONERS CAPTURED today by the XV Corps as follows:-

		Offrs.	O.R.
91st. R.I.R.	1st Bn.	1	227
16th. Bav. Regt.	3rd Bn.		204
LEHR Regt.	2nd Bn.	1	43
	3rd Bn.		3
190th Regt	2nd Bn.		6
	3rd Bn.	3	51
185th Regt	2nd Bn.		6
184th Regt	1st Bn.		2
	2nd Bn.		40
	3rd Bn.		3
185th Pioneer Coy.			1
274th Pioneer Coy.			1
117th Regt.	1st Bn.		5
165th Regt.	3rd Bn.		1
9th M.G.S. Sec.			1
106th M.G.S.Sec.			1
Guard Fusilier Regt	1st Bn.		25
3rd San. Coy.			3
38th San. Coy.			1
39th San. Coy.			18
5th Guard Field Artly. Regt.		1	
183rd Field Artly Regt.		1	[illegible]
		7	64[illegible]
In field ambulances			4
Total		7	6[illegible]

Total to date captured by XV Corps

72	4.448

XV Corps (I)

14th. July 1916.

PRISONERS CAPTURED TODAY by the XV Corps as follows:-

Regiment.	Battn.	Offrs.	O.R.
16th Bav I.R.	1st.	-	7
	2nd.	-	1
	3rd.	2	39
	Stab	-	4
M.G.87 S.S.(16th Bav)		-	1
Guard Fusr.Recruten Depot Coy.		-	2
91st. R.I.R.	1st.	4	31
184th. I.R.	2nd.	-	8
	3rd.	-	3
5th Guard Res. Foot Artly Regt.		-	2
1 Batty Foot A. Bn. 44 (28th R.Div.)		1	2
12th Res. F.A.R.	8th Btty.	-	2
190th I.R.	1st.	3	77
	2nd.	-	5
	3rd.	1	13
165th I.R.	2nd.	1	3
	3rd.	-	4
LEHR Regt.	2nd	-	2
	3rd	-	5
26th I.R.	1st	1	17
	2nd	1	1
	3rd	1 (MC)	65
9th Grenadier Regt	2nd Bn.	-	3
163rd I.R.	2nd	1	0
55th Lw. Ersartz Bn.		-	1
		16	298
In field ambulances			121
	Total	16	419

Total to date captured by XV Corps

88   4,867

Fourth Army, up to 7 p.m. yesterday 14th, has captured a total number of prisoners of 154 officers, 8,900 men.

XV Corps (I).

15th July 1816.

XV CORPS INTELLIGENCE SUMMARY
Covering the period from 7.30 p.m. the 15th inst
to 7.30 p.m. the 16th inst.

The number of prisoners which have passed through cage is as under:-

(a). Corps cage during the last 24 hours ending 7.30 p.m. today 0 officers, 57 Other ranks (Including 48 in field ambulances).

(b). Total taken by the Corps ending 7.30 p.m. today, 88 officers, 4,924 other ranks.

(c). Total taken by the Army up to 7.30 p.m. yesterday, 177 officers, 9,424 other ranks.

OPERATIONS.
During the day our troops have been engaged in consolidating and improving their position.

IDENTIFICATIONS.
During the past 24 hours the following units have been identified:-

	Place where captured.	Number. Offrs.	O.R.
8th DIVISION. 93rd I.R. 3rd Bn.	HIGH WOOD.		1
185th DIVISION 190th I.R. 3rd Bn.	BAZENTIN LE GRAND WOOD (in dugout).		1
3rd GUARD DIVISION 9th Grenadiers 2nd Bn.	S.W. end of HIGH WOOD.		2
10th BAV DIVISION. 16th Bav. Regt erd Bn.	S.W. end of HIGH WOOD.		1
7th DIVISION 165th Regt 3rd Bn. 26th Regt 3rd Bn.	HIGH WOOD		1 1
2nd GUARD RES. DIV. 91st R.I.R. 1st Bn.	N. of BAZENTIN LE GRAND		2
			9
	In field ambulances		48
	Total		57

ENEMY ARTILLERY ACTIVITY.
The enemy artillery has been fairly active and a number of batteries from BOULEAUX WOOD have been firing into CATERPILLAR WOOD and our trenches in front of the BAZENTIN VILLAGES.

PRISONERS STATEMENTS.

(1) A prisoner of the 2nd Bn 9th Grenadier Regt. captured in HIGH WOOD yesterday afternoon. Had been resting in LE MESNIL but had received no reinforcements. He described HIGH WOOD as fairly open but trees lying about.

(2) A prisoner of the 1st Bn, 91st R.I.R. was taken North of BAZENTIN LE GRAND.

He has been in BUCQUOY employed in connection with telephone work but was brought up two days ago. He thinks that other battalions of Regt are in BUCQUOY. He thinks that the 77th and 15th R.I.Rs. are on his right.

He states that guns of the 20th Foot Artillery Regt have arrived also Bavarian Heavy Artillery.

There is a telephone exchange of considerable importance in BUCQUOY.

(3) A prisoner of the 3rd Bn. 26th I.R. arrived two days ago but lost his battalion. He was with the 9th Grenadier Regt.

(4) A prisoner of the 2nd Battn, 9th Grenadier Regt. was taken at Cross roads (S.4.d.). Was taken prisoner yesterday afternoon and had been in wood for one night. He states there is a machine gun at S.4.a.5.7. He states that men of the 26th I.R. are E. of wood.

(5) A prisoner of the 3rd bn, 93rd. I.R., was also captured. Taken at S. 3.b.9.7. Prisoner is very stupid. He arrived here on the 14th. and went into trenches. Has not seen other regts of his division (72nd or 153rd).

Regt has only one M.G.Coy.

Says there are M.Gs. on N.W. side of HIGH WOOD, but cannot say exactly where as he has never been in the wood.

Says there are M.Gs in trench just to right of where he was taken.

<u>NEW TRENCH</u>.

The trench running from X.10.d.40.30 to X.11.b.80.95 has been named BLACK WATCH ALLEY.

C Russell

XV Corps (I).

16th July 1916.

Captain,

General Staff (I).

XV CORPS SUMMARY OF INFORMATION.

BRITISH FRONT. 15th July. Heavy fighting has continued all day in the POZIERES - GUILLEMONT Sector of the German 2nd line of defence, as the result of which further important successes have been gained by our troops. Eastward of LONGUEVAL, in spite of the desperate resistance of the enemy, we have captured the whole of DELVILLE WOOD and have repulsed a strong counter attack with severe losses to the enemy. North of BAZENTIN LE GRAND, our troops have penetrated the German 3rd line at the BOIS de FOUREAUX, in which we have obtained a lodgment. In this neighbourhood a detachment of the enemy were successfully accounted for by a squadron of Dragoon Guards, the first opportunity for mounted action which has been afforded to our cavalry since 1914. West of BAZENTIN LE PETIT we have captured the whole of the wood of that name and have repulsed two counter attacks. Here, amongst other prisoners, we captured a Commander of a Bavarian Regt. with his whole staff. East of OVILLERS a further advance has been made and our troops have fought their way to the outskirts of POZIERES.

During the past 48 hours our aeroplanes have been much hampered by unfavourable weather, and throughout the whole of the 14th the clouds were seldom at a higher altitude than 500 feet.

Despite this drawback, much valuable work has been done. In one of our bombing raids an enemy train was derailed and a coach overturned, while in aerial combats during the last 24 hours we destroyed 3 Fokkers, 3 Biplanes and a double-engined aeroplane, and forced another Fokker to land in a damaged condition. All our machines returned safely to our lines.

FRENCH FRONT. 15th July 1916. On the SOMME the situation remains unchanged. In the VERDUN area there was great artillery artillery in the sector FLEURY.

ITALIAN THEATRE. 14th July. The enemy attack on MONTE MAJO (1) was repulsed.

In the TOFANA MASSIF (2) the Italians successfully sprang a mine and occupied a strong enemy post.

Elsewhere the situation was normal.

(1) MONTE MAJO : 1 miles N. by W. of POSINA.
(2) TOFANA MASSIF: 4 miles W. by N. of CORTINA.

RUSSIAN THEATRE. 15th July. S.W. of RIGA the Germans made several unsuccessful attacks.

N.E. of BARANOWICZY (1) very heavy fighting is reported. The Germans took the offensive and made repeated attacks on the Russian positions. The Russians claimed a slight advance as the result of successful counter attacks.

(1) BARANOWCZY - 30 miles E. by N. of SLONIM.

XV Corps (I).

16th July 1916.

See Lewey

TRANSLATION OF DOCUMENTS.

Extract from order by Lt. Col. KUMME, commanding LEHR Regt. (Date probably 13-7-16).

(1). Maj. v. KRIEGSHEIM will arrange for the relief of his battalion by Herr. v. TSCHIRNHAUS and will march his relieved battalion to FLERS.

Maj. v. ESEBECK will also arrange for the march of rest of his battalion.

(2). In FLERS Maj. v. KRIEGSHEIM, who will represent me, will arrange for the reconstruction of the battalion, the adding of drafts, and division of officers from both battalions. It is to be borne in mind that apart from the staff the 2nd Battn has no officers left.

(3). I will remain in BAZENTIN LE PETIT and continue the fight.

A translation of a Brigade order of the 6th Guard Infantry Brigade, 3rd Guard Division, shows that the 2nd and 3rd Battns of the Lehr Regt are withdrawn to FLERS to act as Brigade reserve and to receive drafts. Date of order 13-7-16.

Captured German Regimental order. Dated 9-7-16.
Read out to 5th Coy., Res. Inf. Regt No. 122.

(1). I intend to strengthen the battalions by the incorporation of drafts from the recruit depot. Detailed returns of the fighting strength of the battalions and of their ration requirements must therefore be submitted without delay in the usual form.

(2). I express my heartiest thanks to the officers in the front line for the splendid manner in which they have in every way kept me abreast of developments by their reports. Thanks to this, the Regt. has so far been spared all surprises.

Also I must thank the men for their exemplary conduct during the strenuous days we have of late passed through.

Nothing has affected that, not even the regrettable way in which the 2nd Battn has been imperilled by the fire of our own artillery. This incident has been made by me the subject of rigorous and strict inquiry, especially the resulting loss of the lives of faithful comrades.

God grant that the offensive power of our greatest enemies in this war may also in the future be stayed by our resistance.

(Signed) KUMML.

Note by G.H.Q.

This is interesting. It shows:-

(1). That the losses of the battalions necessitated the breaking up of the depots close behind the line.

(2). That the German artillery has been shelling its own infantry.

Extracts from the diary of Lt. WINTERMAYER, 8th Coy, 2nd Battn, 16th Bav. I.R. Dated 12-7-16.

Yesterday 6th and today 5th Coy (on the left) dugouts with occupants were knocked about. 5th brings part of its men down into the trench joinging up II/16th with 51st R.I.R. In TRONES WOOD situation not yet cleared up. It is to be retaken tonight. HARDECOURT in enemy hands. Left of GUILLEMONT a battalion was taken out and put into MAMETZ WOOD, for which there has been hard fighting since yesterday. Our 3rd Battn which is there is said to have lost enormously. The 11th Coy lost about 110 men. Fourteen officer casualties. Tonight heavy bombardment of place. O.K's on chateau. Church tower shot away.

In the night 10th-11th on patrol towards BRIQUETERIE before MONTAUBAN.

Tonight English attacked TRONES WOOD. We also were attacked. Had to help 7/16th with my platoon. A meal. Bombardment of 7/16th with all calibres.

It was given out that a fort was captured at VERDUN, that the French had been repulsed S. of SOMME.

We are to be relieved by the 16th in any case.

Four Army Corps are marching up.

XV Corps (I).

16th July 1916.

XV CORPS DAILY INTELLIGENCE SUMMARY
Covering the period from 7.30 p.m. 16th inst
to 7.30 p.m. the 17th inst.

.TROPHIES.

The trophies captured since July 1st. and reported up to noon yesterday by the Fourth Army are as follows:-

21 c.m. Howitzers	5)	These are in
15 c.m. ,,	3)	MAMETZ and
6" Guns (taken at LIEGE)	4)	BAZENTIN Woods.
Assorted guns (calibre unknown)	4	
5.5 c.m. guns (Belgian small)	1	
Field guns (77 m.m. & 10.2 hows)	37	
Automatic Rifles	14	
Machine guns	52	
Minenwerfer (assorted)	30	
Searchlights	2	

The trophies captured by the XV Corps and reported to date are as follows:-

12 c.m. Guns	4
15 c.m. Guns	3
15 c.m. Howitzers	4
21 c.m. Howitzers	2
7.7 c.m. Guns	10
Naval Gun	1
Light Field Gun	1
Machine Guns	33
Automatic Rifles	7
Trench Mortars	6
Minenwerfer	4
Canister Throwers	9
Searchlights	2

PRISONERS.

The number of prisoners who have passed through cages is as under:-

(a). Corps cage during the last 24 hours ending 7.30 p.m. today ..... None.
Wounded prisoners through field ambulances ..... 44.
(b). Total taken by the Corps ending 7.30 p.m. today ..... 88 Officers, 4,968 other ranks.
(c). Total taken by the Fourth Army up to 7.30 p.m. yesterday .... 180 Officers 9,658 other ranks.

AIR RECONNAISSANCE.

The weather has been entirely unfavourable during the past 24 hours.

On the 15th instant our airman were very successful in attacking hostile infantry and transport.

Whenever suitable targets were observed our airmen came down from about 5,000 feet to 2,500 feet and engaged the target.

Lt. Miller, pilot and Lt Short, observer, seeing that our cavalry patrols were being held up by hostile machine gun fire, flew over and engaged the enemy in order to point out to our cavalry where the machine gun fire was coming from. The enemy fire was drawn successfully and each time the enemy fired at our aeroplanes our infantry were able to advance. This was repeated six times.

Capt. Evans and Lt. Long fired on and scattered the remains of a Bn. who were entering LE TRANSLOY.

Capt. Swart and Capt. Wyncoll attacked and scattered a detachment in FLERS, and a detachment on the FLERS - LONGUEVAL Road causing several casualties. There a small party of about 20 men was fired on and 2 were seen to fall. The next to be attacked were three supply wagons, a horse being killed, the wagons hit and hurriedly abandoned by their occupants. The remainder of the ammunition was expended upon a gun limber which was hit.

Lt. Bowen and 2/Lt. Mansell attacked a party of about 50 infantry on the LES BOEUFS - FLERS Road from 2,500 feet dispersing them, a few being left lying on the road. Some men were fired on in GUEUDECOURT and scattered. Transport was damaged on the GINCHY LES BOEUFS Road.

Men were attacked in FLERS and some cavalry who were hiding under trees on the LE BAQUE-FLERS Road were forced to retreat.

All these attacks took place under very heavy A.A. and M.G. fire.

The Buckingham tracer ammunition was used and was easily seen until the ammunition hit the ground.

DISTRIBUTION OF THE ENEMY'S FORCES.

Units fighting North of the SOMME.

IV Corps. Prisoners of the 3rd Bn. 26th Inf. Regt. and of the 3rd Bn. 165th Inf. Regt. (7th Division) were captured N. of BAZENTIN on the night of the 15/16th July.

Prisoners of the following units of the 8th Division were captured on the 16th July N.E. of LONGUEVAL.

1st Bn. 72nd Inf. Regt.
3rd Bn. 93rd Inf. Regt.
2nd Bn. 153rd Inf. Regt.

Prisoners state that they left the LENS front on the 3rd July and marched back to FLINES (N.E.of DOUAI), where they rested three days. They then marched from FLINES via DOUAI to FLERS, where they arrived on the morning of the 15th July. The march was conducted mostly at night.

Prisoners state that the 74th and 75th Field Artillery Regiments are present.

The Div. Cavalry did not accompany them.

The 1st Bn. 72nd, and the 2nd Bn. 153rd Regts. entered the fight at 11.30 a.m. on the 15th inst., and made a counter attack on DELVILLE Wood, which we successfully repulsed.

The 153rd Regt. was relieved in the LENS area by the 9th Bav. Regt., II Bav. Corps.

It appears probable that the IV Corps has been replaced in the line by the IX Res. Corps extending its flank Northwards and the II Bav. Corps Southwards, with the addition of some other units.

A prisoner captured by the 1st Army on the night 15/16th inst. stated he saw Bavarians in the sector held by the IV Corps with "8" on their shoulder straps.

This points possibly to the 8th Bav. Res. Regt. (10th Bav. Div.) having been transferred to this part of the front.

The whole of the 7th Division have been identified North of the SOMME on the 14th and 15th July, it may be assumed that the whole of the IV Corps has been transfered here from the LENS sector.

A prisoner of the 93rd Inf Regt states that all 3 Battns of his Regt are in front line.

2nd Guard Reserve Division. A deserter of the 2nd Battn, 77th. Res. Regt. surrendered on the 16th July W. of BAZENTIN LE PETIT. He states that the 1st Battn of his Regt is on his left and the 55th Res Regt on his right, with the 15th Res Regt. still further West.

It appears that the whole of the 2nd Guard Res. Div. has been moved South to the POZIERES - BAZENTIN sector. It is not known what unit has taken its place between HANNESCAMPS and GOMMECOURT, but it is probably one of the divisions which suffered heavily in the early days of the battle, e.g. the 26th. Res. Div.

CASUALTIES.

A diary belonging to Oberst Leutnant REDALL, Commanding the 16th Bav. Regt. gives the following losses suffered by the 3 Bns. of his Regt. between July 1st and 12th :-

Officers	6 killed	14 wounded
Other ranks	126 ,,	642 ,,
		72 missing
		5 gassed
		15 sick

Total number of casualties 880.

It is interesting to note that during this period we only captured 16 men belonging to this Regt, hence, out of the 72 missing 56 must have been killed.

Since the 12th inst we have taken prisoner 5 officers and 340 men, including the regimental commander and a Bn commander. Hence the known casualties up to date are

	killed	wounded	Missing & sick.	TOTAL.
Officers	6	14	5	25
Other ranks	182	662	356	1,200

The above total necessarily omits those men killed and wounded since the 12th inst which must have been large, as our bombardment of the line held by this regt greatly increased from that date.

INFORMATION REGARDING PLACES BEHIND ENEMY LINES.

From the examination of prisoners and captured documents, the following places are of importance to the enemy:-

(a) FLERS Village - A former divisional H.Q. and the centre of the D.R.L.S. Probably still a regimental H.Q. and billets of supporting troops.

(b) FAUCOURT L'ABBAYE - A strong point and probably a big ammunition or supply dump judging from the amount of traffic constantly seen visiting this place.

(c) The farm surrounded by trees in M.21.a.S.W. of LE SARS is probably an ammunition or supply dump (marked on German map).

(d) XIV Corps Headquarters - BEUGNY.

Other Headquarters -
(GUEUDECOURT.
(LE TRANSLOY.
(BARASTRE.
(SOEMILLE (W. of ROUSSOY).
(TEMPLEUX.
(SAILLY-SAILLISEL.

(e) An ammunition park in the park N.17.b. BEAULENCOURT.

(f) The cross roads at N.19.c.8.0 are used a great deal.

(g) The roads:- FLERS - GUEUDECOURT.
,, - LE SARS.
,, - GINCHY.
,, - MARTINPUICH.

are certain to be constantly used at night for supplies and reliefs.

(h) The S.W. corner of HAVRINCOURT WOOD where smoke has been twice reported to have been seen.

(i) From a captured German document all transport drivers are warned that they must be thoroughly acquainted with the following roads:- MAUREPAS - LE FOREST - RANCOURT - MOISLAINS - AIZECOURT LE HAUT to TEMPLEUX LE FOSSE.

(j) Civilians and prisoners of war are being sent to EPEHY, MOISLAINS, ROISEL, TEMPLEUX LE GUERARD.

(k) The following are of importance:-
Pioneer Park at COMBLES.
Supply depot at "
Ammunition depot " (believed detroyed)
Supply Depot at BOUCHAVESNES

(l) There is water main with stations for drawing water at the N.W. edge of MARTINPUICH also at FLERS.

ENEMY ARTILLERY ACTIVITY.

There was heavy shelling chiefly with H.E. of BAZENTIN LE GRAND and BAZENTIN LE PETIT WOODS.

A few 77 m.m. only were fired into MAMETZ WOOD and district.

There was no shelling of MAMETZ, FRICOURT or the rest of our back area.

G Russell

Captain,

General Staff (I).

XV Corps (I).

17th July 1916.

Copy of G.H.Q. No. O.A.D. 69 dated 15.7.16.

The attack carried out so successfully by the Fourth Army yesterday reflects the highest credit on the Commanders and Staffs who planned and arranged it and on the troops of all ranks who executed it with such vigour and bravery.

It was a very fine feat of arms and has opened the way to further successes.

I congratulate you and all under your command very warmly not only on what you have already achieved but on the vigorous efforts being made to develop to the utmost the very favourable opportunities opened up by your success.

---

21 Div.
G. 137.

The above copy of G.H.Q. letter No. O.A.D. 69 of 15.7.16 from the Commander-in-Chief, is forwarded for your information and communication to all concerned.

H.G. Franklyn Maj
for. Lieut.Colonel
G.S. 21 Div

16.7.16.

Distribution.	Copies.
62 Inf. Bde.	10
64 " "	10
110 " "	10
Div. Art.	25
Div. Eng.	4
Pioneers.	1
Signals.	2
178 Tun. Co.	1
Div. Train.	5
F[illegible]s.	3
S[illegible] Sec.	1
M[illegible] Vet.Sec.	1
Supply Col.	1
Salvage Co.	1
"Q"	1
C.Comdt.	1
A.D.M.S.	1
A.D.V.S.	1
A.P.M.	1
D.[illegible]D.O.S.	1

S P E C I A L   O R D E R.

by Major-General D.G.M.Campbell, C.B., Comdg. 21st Division.

I cannot too strongly express to all ranks my intense admiration for their splendid gallantry in actually breaking through the German first and second lines.

No Division has a finer performance to its credit.

Until, however, the high ground North of the German second line has been seized and consolidated, we cannot consider our work complete.

Although I fully recognise the tremendous strain which has been imposed on all ranks, I am confident, after their previous magnificent performances, that I can absolutely rely on them to answer any call that may be made upon them until they have wrested their final objective from the enemy.

David G M Campbell

Major-General,
Commanding 21st Division.

18th July, 1916.

This order to be read to all troops and then destroyed.

FOR WAR DIARY

Fourth Army No. 266 (G).

21st Division.

Owing to the difficulty of assembling the Division it will not be possible for me to address them personally as I had wished.

I desire, therefore, that my congratulations and thanks may be conveyed to each Officer, N.C.O., and man of the Division for their excellent work and great gallantry during the Battle of the SOMME.

Their two successful assaults against the carefully prepared defences of the enemy's first and second systems is a feat of arms which will rank high in the attainments of the British Army.

No troops could have answered to the call of duty with greater dash, and the valour of the infantry, coupled with the excellent support afforded by the artillery, is deserving of the highest praise.

Your Corps Commander has repeatedly expressed to me his satisfaction both with the training of the Division before the first assault, and the behaviour of all ranks when in close contact with the enemy.

I regret that the 21st Division is leaving the Fourth Army, but they performed their part in this great battle in a manner that has filled me with admiration, and I trust that at some future time I may again have the honour of finding them under my command.

H Rawlinson

General,
Commanding Fourth Army.

H.Q. Fourth Army.
21st July, 1916.

Relief of 6th D.C.L.I. in Quarters

1. Relief will commence at 5 p.m. from Billets. Platoons will move off at 3 minutes interval in following order. A Coy. D Coy. B Coy. C Coy. Headqrs Details.
The whole will march up [illegible] Ave & will be guided by guides from the D.C.L.I. These guides will report at Barracks at 4-30 p.m. (1 guide for each platoon)

2. Carrying Parties – Each Coy will provide 40 men carrying parties who will march with the rear platoon of each Coy. These men may carry up anything which would be required before the arrival of the Transport, probably at midnight.

3. Officers Mess will be ready for loading in Entrance Hall at Bn. H.Q. at 4-45 p.m. together with Officers kits etc not carried up by carrying parties. Boxes from the Coys, Orderly Room boxes will be collected at the Barracks at 4-45 p.m.
1 Officers servant per Coy will remain with Mess etc. & 1 cook per Coy will remain with the boxes to load up. Transport will

call at H.Q. & the Bombers will. Take the Stores to the Batn. Bomb Store situated about 100 yards in rear of Candle Factory.

4/ Carrying parties. O.B. Coy will supply ration carriers for themselves & the Coy which they support.

Ration parties will be relieved at Batn H.Q. if possible.

5/ D. Coy will take over Crest 98 & 99
C " " " " " 100 & 101.
A " " be in support of C Coy.
B " " " " " " D. "

[illegible] Capt & Adjt
1-(S) Bn [illegible] Regt.

SECRET. Copy No. 6.

110th INFANTRY BRIGADE OPERATION ORDER NO. 29.

26. 7. 16.

1. The 110th Brigade will take over trenches from the 43rd Infantry Brigade in J.2. Sector on the 28th July in accordance with preliminary instructions issued on the 25th inst.

2. The Brigade(less 7th Bn. Leic. Regt.) will billet in ARRAS on the night of the 27th/28th July.

3. Units will move to a place just EAST of WANQUETIN on the 27th inst. as follows:-

6th Battn. Leic. Regt. by lorries leaving LIENCOURT STATION at 10 a.m.

The 8th and 9th Bns. Leic. Regt. and 110th M. G. Coy. by march route in foregoing order, head of 8th Battn. to pass cross roads at South end of LATTRE-St.-QUENTIN at 2 pm.

A 21st Divisional Staff Officer will show the 6th Bn. where they will halt for the day, also ground for 8th and 9th Bns. Leic. Regt. and 110th M. G. Coy.

The 6th Bn. Leic. Regt. will arrange for guides to show these units their ground on their arrival.

4. The Brigade (less 7th Bn. Leic. Regt.) will march from halting place East of WANQUETIN to ARRAS.

Order of march - 6th, 8th, 9th Bns. Leic. Regt., 110th M. G. Coy. 6th Battn. to leave at 7.30 p.m.

200 yards distance will be kept between companies.

The head of the 6th Bn. will not pass under the Railway Bridge West of DAINVILLE until 9 p.m.

5. Three buses will leave LIENCOURT STATION at 10 a.m. 27th inst. calling at Church, LATTRE-St.-QUENTIN at 10.45 a.m. These will convey the Machine Gun Teams of the 110th M. G. Coy. and Lewis Gun Teams of the 8th and 9th Battns. who are taking over from the 43rd Brigade, to the Railway Bridge West of DAINVILLE, where guides of the 43rd Infantry Brigade will meet them at 1 p.m. and conduct them to the trenches. Teams will take their guns complete.

The 8th Bn. will detail 1 Officer and 1 N.C.O. to go by these buses to take over Stokes Mortar emplacements, and all ammunition in the Sector to be taken over by the 110th Brigade. They will rejoin their unit on the night of the 27/28 inst. in ARRAS.

6. Billeting parties from each unit will proceed by buses referred to in para 5 and will report to the Town Major ARRAS in the RUE VICTOR HUGO at 5 p.m. These billeting parties will send guides to meet their units at the CHAPELLE du St. SACREMONT (at West entrance to ARRAS) at 9.30 p.m. 27th inst.

7. The Headquarters and 3 Companies of the 6th Battn. Leic. Regt. and details of 110th M. G. Coy. will take over billets now occupied by 10th Durham L.I. and 43rd M. G. Coy. respectively on evening of 28th inst. Arrangements to be made by Commanding Officers concerned.

8. Units will take over trenches in accordance with Preliminary Orders issued on 25th inst. as follows :-

110th M. G. Coy. during 27th inst. under Coy. arrangements

<u>28th inst.</u>
9th Bn. Leic. Regt. leave their billets at 4 p.m.
8th " " " " " " " 5 "
1 Coy. 6th Bn. Leic. Regt. " " " 6 "

The above to move by platoons at 3 minutes interval.

The 6th D.C.L.I. and 10th D.L.I. will have guides at 43rd Brigade H.Q. one hour before the above times.

The 9th, 8th, and 6th Bns. Leic. Regt. will send guides to 43rd Bde. H. Q. one hour before moving off to conduct 43rd Bde. guides to their respective billets.

All details of relief will be arranged by Commanding Officers concerned.

9. The 7th Battn. Leic. Regt. will march from BEAUFORT to AGNEZ-LES-DUISANS on the 28th inst. where they will be billeted. March to be completed by 12 noon.

The Battn. will be in Divisional Reserve.

10. Until futher orders, the 110th M. G. Coy. will leave one section in transport camp in Divisional Reserve.

11. The transport of the 6th, 8th, and 9th Bns. Leic. Regt. and 110th M. G. Coy. will camp from the night of the 27/28th inst. at MONTENESCOURT, Place will be notified later.

12. Units will report on completion of relief.

13. Lists of trench stores taken over will be forwarded to Brigade H.Q. by 8 p.m. 29th inst.

14. Bde. H. Q. will close at LIENCOURT at 2 p.m. 28th inst. and open at Headquarters now occupied by 43rd Brigade at 4 p.m.

A W Fletcher
Major,
Brigade Major, 110th Brigade.

Issued at 6.30 a.m. 27.7.16.

Copy No. 1 21st Div. G.
" " 2 " " Q.
" " 3 43rd Inf. Bde.
" " 4 6th Bn.Leic. Regt.
" " 5 7th " " "
" " 6 8th " " "
" " 7 9th " " "
" " 8 110th M. G. Coy.
" " 9 Bde. Transport Officer.
" " 10 - 12 Office.

6TH. (SERVICE) BATTALION DUKE OF CORNWALL'S LIGHT INFANTRY.

SECRET. OPERATION ORDER NO. 20. COPY NO. 11

1. The Battalion will be relieved by the 8th and 9th Leicesters tomorrow, 28th. inst.

2. O. C. Coys will send one guide per platoon to be at Brigade Headquarters at 2. 45p.m tomorrow. These men must know the number of their trench or name of work.

3. O. C. Coys will detail a party of one N. C. O. and 5 men to remain behind and accompany Transport.

4. Officers Trench Kits to be at Candle Factory by 5. 30p.m. I servant per Company to remain behind with trench Kits.

5. Men are to fill their Water Bottles before relief.

6. The Battalion will be billeted at SUCRERIE, L.10.B., LOUEZ.

7. During daylight Companies will march with 100 yards distance between Platoons.

8. Trench Maps and log books to be handed to reliefs, by Companies, together with S.A.A. Trench Stores and Grenades.

9. All dugouts, latrines etc., are to be left scrupulously clean and creosoled.

(Sd) F. C. Harrison, 2/Lieutenant,
A/Adjutant 6th. Battalion D. C. L. I.

27th. July 1916.

Copy No. 1. Orderly Room.
2. A. Coy.
3. B. Coy.
4. C. Coy.
5. D. Coy.
6. Bombers.
7. Lewis Gunners.
8. Signallers.
9. Transport Officer.
10. C. O.
11. Adjutant.

M A P S .

MONTAUBAN.
PARTS OF SHEETS 57D S.E., 57C S.W. 62D N.E., 62C N.W.
Contalmaison
Longueval
Montauban
Mametz
Fricourt
Guillemont
La Boisselle
Bernafay Wood
Bazentin le Grand
Delville Wood
Carnoy
Hardecourt
BRITISH FRONT LINE
REFERENCE.
Scale 1 : 20,000
TRENCHES CORRECTED TO 2-6-16.

TRENCH MAP.

MONTAUBAN.

Scale 1:20,000.

MONTAUBAN

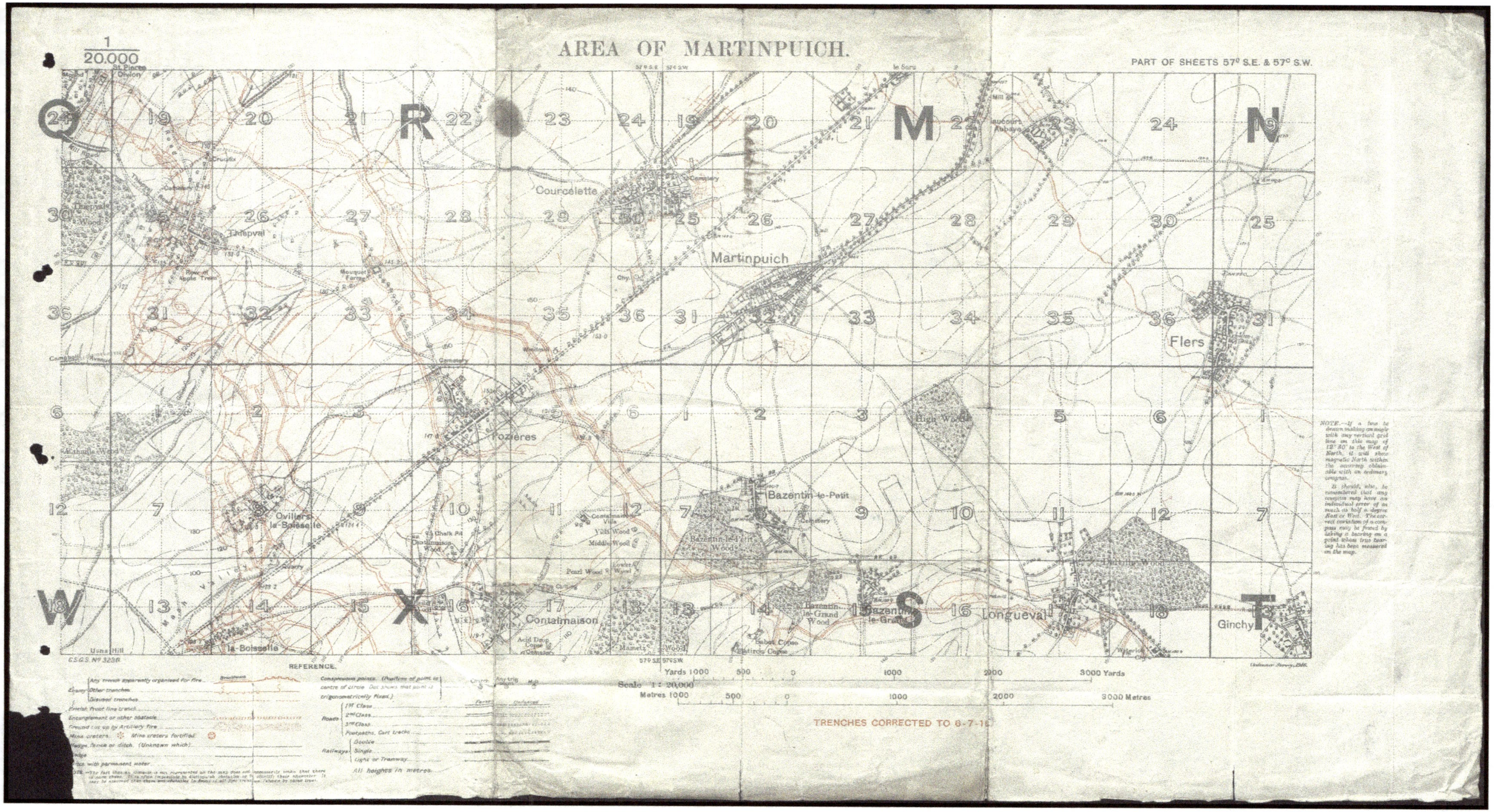
AREA OF MARTINPUICH.
1/20,000
PART OF SHEETS 57° S.E. & 57° S.W.
Courcelette
Martinpuich
Flers
Thiepval
Pozières
Bazentin-le-Petit
High Wood
Ovillers-la-Boisselle
Contalmaison
Bazentin-le-Grand
Longueval
Ginchy
La Boisselle
Scale 1: 20,000
TRENCHES CORRECTED TO 8-7-16
All heights in metres.
REFERENCE.

TRENCH MAP.

AREA OF

MARTINPUICH.

Scale 1 : 20,000.

MARTINPUICH

110th Brigade.

21st Division.

1/8th BATTALION

LEICESTERSHIRE REGIMENT

AUGUST 1916.

Instructions regarding War Diaries and Intelligence Summaries are contained in F. S. Regs., Part II. and the Staff Manual respectively. Title Pages will be prepared in manuscript.

WAR DIARY
or
INTELLIGENCE SUMMARY
(Erase heading not required.)

Army Form C. 2118.

Vol 11

21/1111

8th Bn Lincolnshire Regt

Place	Date	Hour	Summary of Events and Information	Remarks and references to Appendices
1-8-16 Trenches (98-101)			Our dispositions are as follows. "C" and "D" Coys in front line trenches, "B" Coy in Support and "C" Coy in reserve AAA The enemy shelled our sectors rather heavily between 12.30 and 2 pm. The shells used were chiefly 5.9" and whizbangs AAA About 63 shells fell on sectors (97–101), but very little damage was done. The enemy put up an observation balloon at mid-day, which remained up until dusk.	
2-8-16			Relief of Companies took place as per enclosed schedule AAA About 2.45 pm yesterday an enemy aeroplane appeared over our lines, and appeared to drop a smoke bomb over ROCLINCOURT AAA It flew very low, and our artillery opened fire on it, but without success. The night passed off very quietly	
3-8-16			At 12.30 pm a fleet of aeroplanes passed over our lines, flying towards the enemy trenches AAA At 1 pm 21 were observed to return, one being damaged, but it landed safely behind our lines AAA About 2 pm one of the enemy's shells appeared to have caused a fire behind ROCLINCOURT, column of smoke going in the air for about 10 minutes. At 3.30 pm enemy fired several shells into ARRAS. The Companies in the front line trenches worked on new dug-outs which are being constructed.	
4-8-16			An explosion occurred at 11.25 am this morning at the "fork roads" close to the R.E. dump AAA It is believed that an enemy whizbang dropped on a dump of French bombs and Rifle Grenades AAA Our Battn Pioneers were in a cellar underneath the house but they escaped without injury except 2 who were slightly wounded. The day passed off very quietly in the trenches.	

2449 Wt. W14957/M90 750,000 1/16 J.B.C. & A. Forms/C.2118/12.

Army Form C. 2118.

WAR DIARY
or
INTELLIGENCE SUMMARY
(Erase heading not required.)

Instructions regarding War Diaries and Intelligence Summaries are contained in F. S. Regs., Part II. and the Staff Manual respectively. Title Pages will be prepared in manuscript.

8th Bn Leicestershire Regt 2

Place	Date	Hour	Summary of Events and Information	Remarks and references to Appendices
5-8-16 Trenches (98-101)			The enemy ~~appeared to~~ put up what appeared to be a new kind of observation balloon, opposite our sector AAA It consisted of a series of 8 balloons on a rope or chain AAA It remained up until after dusk. At about 4.15 pm our own artillery fired into our trenches, 4 shells dropping just behind our front line Trench 101 AAA This luckily caused no damage, and may have been caused through the gunners firing a new gun AAA	
6-8-16			Work was continued on dug-outs and traverses AAA Enemy artillery were fairly active throughout the day, and about 5.30 pm some heavy shells dropped in the support Trenches AAA No damage was done. Our artillery replied effectively AAA About 6.30 pm a fleet of aeroplanes passed over our lines in the direction of those of the enemy. They were observed to return about 8 pm.	
7-8-16			Enemy very quiet during the day AAA About 9 pm our artillery opened a lively cannonade on the enemy trenches AAA This continued for about half an hour. The Battalion were relieved by the 6th Bn Leicestershire Regt. Orders for relief see schedule enclosed. After being relieved the Battalion marched in companies to AGNEZ-LES-DUISANS a distance of about 9 kilometres, arriving there about midnight While at AGNEZ-LES-DUISANS, the Battalion were in Divisional Reserve	
8-8-16 Agnez les Duisans			The morning was spent in kit inspections etc The signallers and Battalion Raiders returned to companies for duty. During the ~~B~~ afternoon the Battalion were engaged in bathing parades.	

2449 Wt. W14957/M90 750,000 1/16 J.B.C. & A. Forms/C.2118/12.

Instructions regarding War Diaries and Intelligence Summaries are contained in F. S. Regs., Part II. and the Staff Manual respectively. Title Pages will be prepared in manuscript.

WAR DIARY
or
INTELLIGENCE SUMMARY
(Erase heading not required.)

Army Form C. 2118.

3

8th Bn Leicestershire Regt

Place	Date	Hour	Summary of Events and Information	Remarks and references to Appendices
9-8-16 Agny Les-Duisans			There was an early morning parade under the R.S.M from 6.30 am to 7.15 AM for the Battalion and for all subalterns AAA The new draft were inspected by the C.O. at 9.15 AM AAA The morning was spent in Company and Platoon Drill, Physical Training + Bayonet Fighting. The afternoon was spent in resting, with the exception of the new draft, who were on parade under Sergt Herring.	
10.8.16			Early morning parade for physical drill etc under the RSM. Companies were at the disposal of Company Commanders from 9.15 am to 12.15 am AAA In the afternoon a reconnaissance of the Divisional Area took place by Company Commanders, and one other officer per Company.	
11.8.16			Usual early morning parade under the supervision of the RSM aaa. Special attention was paid on this parade to "saluting" At 8.45 am the Battalion fell in to go on a route march. A Coy moved off at 9am, the remaining Companies in succession at intervals of 15 minutes AAA The route chosen was AGNEZ-LES-DUISANS to cross roads K.6.2.2.8 thence to cross roads K.1.6.8.8 thence to HABARCQ, thence home via LARESSET. Packs were not carried. The Lewis Guns and Stretcher Bearers classes were carried on as usual AAA At 5.30 pm the newly joined officers were on parade under the CO for communication drill	

Instructions regarding War Diaries and Intelligence Summaries are contained in F. S. Regs., Part II. and the Staff Manual respectively. Title Pages will be prepared in manuscript.

WAR DIARY
or
INTELLIGENCE SUMMARY

(Erase heading not required.)

Army Form C. 2118.

8th 4th Bn Leicestershire Regt

Place	Date	Hour	Summary of Events and Information	Remarks and references to Appendices
12-8-16 Agny-les-Duissans			Early morning parade under R.S.M AAA At 11am the G.O.C 21st Divn inspected the Battalion on the Battalion Parade Grounds. Coys fell in at 10.25 am on their markers, specialists parading with their companies. The inspection lasted about an hour.	
13-8-16			There was no usual early morning parade AAA. Church of England parade at 10.30am under Capt Beardsley AAA Roman Catholics Mass 10.30 AM, Parish Church. Other denominations 9am and 11.30am at the School.	
14.8.16			There was the usual early morning parade under the supervision of the RSM, special attention being paid to Physical Drill and Bayonet Fighting AAA During the morning the Battalion were engaged in bathing A Coy 9am to 10am. B Coy 10am to 11am. C Coy 11am to 12am. D Coy 12am to 1pm. Headquarters details ie Lewis Gunners, Signallers, Raiders and Bombers. From 9am to 12 noon, the Battalion Raiders paraded for instruction under 2nd Lt Hugh Jones, the Signallers under 2nd Lt Geo Dixie Smith, and the Lewis Gunners under 2nd Lt Geo Clarke	
15-8-16			RSM's parade 6.30am to 7.15am AAA Company parades during the morning as usual	
16.8.16			Usual early morning parade under RSM. During the morning Staff Sgt Baker of the Bayonet Fighting and Physical Training Staff took the undermentioned classes in Bayonet Fighting on the Battalion Parade ground:– 9am All Platoon Officers 11am N.C.O's and Raiders	

2449 Wt. W14957/M90 750,000 1/16 J.B.C. & A. Forms/C.2118/12.

Instructions regarding War Diaries and Intelligence Summaries are contained in F. S. Regs., Part II. and the Staff Manual respectively. Title Pages will be prepared in manuscript.

WAR DIARY
or
INTELLIGENCE SUMMARY

(Erase heading not required.)

Army Form C. 2118.

5

8th Bn Leicestershire Regt

Place	Date	Hour	Summary of Events and Information	Remarks and references to Appendices
17-8-16 Agnez-les-Duisans			There was no early morning parade. The morning was spent in Interior Economy. The 8th Bn Relieved the 6th Battalion in the trenches. For Details of Relief see schedule enclosed	
18-8-16 Trenches (99-101)			Our dispositions were C & D Coys in the firing line. A+B Coys in support. The day was very quiet, and useful work was done in constructing dug outs and traverses. Towards evening 3 German observation balloons were up opposite our trenches.	
19-8-16			Considerable activity was shown by the enemy in the morning and about 11 am Trench 100 was shelled with 14 7.7 shells, and 21 Medium T.M. Bombs were fired into the same Trench between 5.20 pm and 7.45 pm. Slight damage was done to the trenches but no casualties resulted. Our field guns retaliated on our enemy front line, and our Trench Mortars also carried out effective retaliation against trenches opposite 98/101. The Stokes Guns also did some shooting AAA During the night a patrol went out, to reconnoitre and returned without having encountered any of the enemy.	
20-8-16			Enemy artillery were very active throughout the day AAA About 11 am some very heavy shells were dropped in the vicinity of the Candle Factory, but very little damage was done. At 1.40 pm 4 15 cm T.M. Bombs fell in rear of Trench 98, and again at 7.15 pm the enemy fired 6 heavy T.M. Bombs which fell in rear of Trenches 98-101. Our working parties were engaged in building up the parapets and parados, which were damaged by the enemy artillery yesterday	

2449 Wt. W14957/M90 750,000 1/16 J.B.C. & A. Forms/C.2118/12.

Instructions regarding War Diaries and Intelligence Summaries are contained in F. S. Regs., Part II. and the Staff Manual respectively. Title Pages will be prepared in manuscript.

WAR DIARY
or
INTELLIGENCE SUMMARY
(Erase heading not required.)

Army Form C. 2118.

6

8th Bn Leicestershire Regt

Place	Date	Hour	Summary of Events and Information	Remarks and references to Appendices
21-8-16 Trenches (99-101)			WORK REPORT Wiring round CLARENCE CRATER. Rebuilding damage caused by enemy Trench Mortars to parapets and parados. Deepening and improving HOLBORN VIADUCT. Building up Traverse 96H. Wiring in front of J101. INTELLIGENCE The enemy artillery and Trench Mortars were very active throughout the day. ~~AB~~ During the afternoon numerous shells dropped in and around O WORK and S100. No damage was done. Three 5.9 shells dropped in November Avenue, causing damage to the sides of the trench. During both stand tos enemy machine guns swept the parapets of J100 and J101 AAA At 8AM a few men were seen working in trench opposite Trench 101, but no identification could be made.	
22.8.16			WORK REPORT Deepening S96 Trench. Building up Parados and parapets. Remainder of men working under R.E.s in Dug Out L6. ~~The~~ INTELLIGENCE The enemy artillery and Trench Mortars still continued to be very active, especially between 5pm and 7pm.	
23.8.16			A carefully prepared raid was carried out on the enemy's lines at S6 C40 after a combined bombardment of CHANTECLER and the salient S18A3.1. The bombardment was arranged to spread over 3 days called X, Y + Z, and consisted of 6" + 4.5" Hows, Trench Mortars and 18 pounders, as per particulars and map enclosed. On Z day (23rd) during the bombardment the fire was lifted to the "Support Line" when our "Raiding Party" under 2nd Lt Hugh Jones made for the enemy's front line trench through a gap in the wire which our artillery had made for them	

2449 Wt. W14957/M90 750,000 1/16 J.B.C. & A. Forms/C.2118/12.

Army Form C. 2118.

7

8th Bn Lancashire Regt

Instructions regarding War Diaries and Intelligence Summaries are contained in F. S. Regs., Part II. and the Staff Manual respectively. Title Pages will be prepared in manuscript.

WAR DIARY
or
INTELLIGENCE SUMMARY

(Erase heading not required.)

Place	Date	Hour	Summary of Events and Information	Remarks and references to Appendices
23.8.16			They found the wire deserted, but gained some useful tactical information AAA The party all returned safely.	
24.8.16			During the day the enemy sent over rather frequently heavy Trench Mortars in reply to our artillery. They seem to rely on chiefly on these for retaliation. They still appear to be nervous, and during the night very lights, and red rockets were sent up very frequently. Our working parties in the trenches were chiefly engaged in building up the parapets and traverses, and strengthening the dug outs.	
25.8.16			During the day the enemy had several balloons up, but when our aeroplanes appeared on the scene towards evening they were quickly drawn in AAA Enemy trench mortars were again rather busy but no material damage was done. Enemy snipers were rather active and at 5 pm our "Stokes Guns" fired 12 rounds on enemy snipers post 96 963 from 101 emplacement, with good effect.	
26.8.16			The day and night passed off very quietly. The enemy apparently made no attempt to repair the rents in his wire caused by our bombardment previous to the raid.	

2449 Wt. W14957/M90 750,000 1/16 J.B.C. & A. Forms/C.2118/12.

Instructions regarding War Diaries and Intelligence Summaries are contained in F. S. Regs., Part II. and the Staff Manual respectively. Title Pages will be prepared in manuscript.

WAR DIARY
or
INTELLIGENCE SUMMARY
(Erase heading not required.)

Army Form C. 2118.

8

8th Bn Leicestershire Regt

Place	Date	Hour	Summary of Events and Information	Remarks and references to Appendices
27.8.16			At 1.15 am the sentry in Sap 99 heard a German Patrol in front of them. At 1.20 am the patrol had approached the sap, and a man was seen about 25 yards away, on the edge of the sap (which had been filled in with wire owing to the enemy's mining operations). One of the sentries threw a bomb at this man, seriously wounding him. In the meantime the other sentry had warned the reliefs and Lewis Gunners. The former manned the end of the sap and the latter took up their position in a bay at the foot of the sap. We then sent up a light which revealed about 6 men lying in the grass. Our Lewis Gunners immediately opened fire, Groans were heard and 2nd Lt Clarke and a man went out to investigate AAA A bomb was thrown at them, by a German who was concealed in the grass but luckily it failed to explode, and was afterwards found to be undetonated. 2nd Lt Clarke captured the German and brought him into our trenches. Two men went out to fetch a German in who had been hit by our Lewis Gun fire, but when our men arrived he was found to be dead. Both Germans belonged to the 93rd ANHALT REGT.	
28.8.16			Nothing worth noting happened on this day. The enemy did not put up any observation balloons during the day. Our working parties worked on traverses, and deepening communication trenches.	
29.8.16			The day and night passed off very quietly. The enemy still appear to be very "nervous" and kept sending up numerous very lights during the night. We had a patrol out, which gained some useful information regarding the condition of the enemy's wire etc	

2449 Wt. W14957/M90 750,000 1/16 J.B.C. & A. Forms/C.2118/12.

Instructions regarding War Diaries and Intelligence Summaries are contained in F. S. Regs., Part II. and the Staff Manual respectively. Title Pages will be prepared in manuscript.

WAR DIARY
or
INTELLIGENCE SUMMARY

(Erase heading not required.)

Army Form C. 2118.

9

8th Bn Leicestershire Regt

Place	Date	Hour	Summary of Events and Information	Remarks and references to Appendices
30-8-16			The day passed off very quietly also the night with the exception of a few rifle grenades. An enemy searchlight played round our trenches from a Southerly direction. One of our snipers claims having killed 2 of the enemy during the day.	
31-8-16			The enemy made things fairly lively for CLAUDE and CLARENCE Craters, with Rifle Grenades and Trench Mortars. Between midnight and 1.30 AM, about 50 T.M. fell round 101 Sap, and a traverse on the right was blown in, burying 3 of our men, without injuring them	

[illegible] Lt. Col.
Comdg 8th Leicestershire Regt

RELIEF ORDERS.

The following Reliefs will take place tomorrow August 2nd. 1916

(1) 1 N.C.O. & 12 men C.Coy. will relieve 1 N.C.O. & 12 men A.Coy. Ration Party at Candle Factory directly after Breakfast. The 1 N.C.O. & 12 men A.Coy. will go to Bosky Redoubt.

(2) A.Coy. less 1 Officer & 30 O.R. (left as garrison in Bosky Redoubt) & 1 N.C.O. & 12 men (ration party at Candle Factory) will relieve C.Coy. Trenches 100 & 101 relief to commence at 1p.m.

(3) C.Coy. on being relieved in front line will send 40 O.R. to Bosky Redoubt, 1 N.C.O. & 12 men to relieve 1 N.C.O. & 12 men Ration Party A.Coy. at Candle Factory and remainder to dug-out at Battn. Hdqrs. C.Coy. Hdqrs. will be in Bosky Redoubt.

(4) On C.Coy. garrisoning the redoubt, A.Coy. garrison will move up to the Front Line Trenches, with the exception of the 8 men working in mine dug-out who will not be relieved until 4p.m. by C.Coy.

(5) B.Coy. (less miners at work in Dug-outs in supports) will relieve D.Coy. Trenches 98 & 99 commencing at 2p.m.

(6) D.Coy. on relief will take over the Support Line and will send 2 N.C.O's & 24 men to Candle Factory to relieve the carrying party of 2 N.C.O's &24 men B.Coy. The 2 N.C.O's & 24 men B.Coy. will rejoin their Coy. in Front Line.

(7) A & B Coys. will atke over trench stores etc. in Front Line at 9a.m. C.Coy. will take over Trench Stores etc. in redoubt at 9a.m.

(8) All coys. will report to Battn. Hdqrs. when their reliefs are complete.

(9) The Signalling Officer will arrange for the reliefs of the Signallers. Lewis Gun Teams will be relieved with their Coys.

Capt. & Adjt.
8th. (Ser) Bn. Leicestershire Regt.

OPERATION ORDER NO 39 BY
MAJOR G.C.I.HERVEY, COMMDG.,
8TH (SER) BN. LEICESTERSHIRE REGT. 6-8-16

---

1. RELIEF. The 6th. Battn. will relieve the 8th. Battn. Leicester Regt. in the Trenches tomorrow the 7th. inst. The 8th. Battn. going into Divisional Reserve at AGNEZ-LES-DUISANS.

2. ORDER OF RELIEF. Left Coy. Right Coy. Support Coy. ½ Coy. from Rocky Redoubt and ½ Coy. Battn. reserve at Battn. Hdqrs.
The leading platoon of 6th. Leicesters will pass Candle Factory at about 6-[illegible]p.m. remaining platoons will follow in succession at 3 mins. interval.

3. GUIDES. Each Coy. will send [illegible] guides (2 per platoon) to report to R.S.M. at Candle Factory at 5-45p.m.- These guides will conduct the Platoons of 6th. Leicesters from Candle Factory to the Trenches.

4. ROUTE. Platoons as relieved will march independently under their own guides to AGNEZ-LES-DUISANS via Candle Factory ST NICHOLAS, junction of roads G/.21.b.47 (Map 51b.N.W.3, ST POL ROAD, DUISANS Map 51c.)

5. BILLETS. A billeting party consisting of the Quarter Master and the R.Q.M.S. will take over the Billets at AGNEZ from the 7th. Leicesters before 6p.m. August 7th.

6. BAGGAGE AND STORES. All officers Mess kit & baggage to go by Transport must be taken down to Candle Factory by 6p.m. 1 man per Coy. will remain as guard and will load baggage on arrival of Transport. 1 Cook per Coy. will remain at Candle Factory to load dixies on Transport, the remainder will join their platoons as they pass Candle Factory.

7. SIGNALLERS AND LEWIS GUNNERS. The Signallers and Lewis Gunners will be relieved at about 4p.m. The 6th. Battn. Signallers and Lewis Gunners will have the teas brought up for the 8th. Battn. Lewis Gunners and Signallers in the Trenches, and the 8th. Battn. Signallers and Lewis Gunners will have their teas at Candle Factory when relieved. 1 man per Lewis Gun team will remain at Candle Factory to load up Lewis Gun stores on Transport.

8. TRENCH STORES. Representatives of 6th. Battn. will take over Trench Stores during the afternoon of 7th. inst. (Very Guns Very Pistols, and periscopes will be handed over to relieving Coys)
Copy of Handing over Forms will be sent to Orderly Room by 10a.m. 8th. inst.

9. O.C. Coys. will report to Battn. Hdqrs when their relief is complete.

10. TEAS Tea will be issued to the men on arrival at Billets.

[illegible]

Capt. & Adjt.

8th. (SER) BN. LEICESTERSHIRE REGT.

BM 226/3.1.

SECRET

SPECIAL TASKS FOR ENSUING WEEK.

A combined bombardment of CHANTECLER and the Salient G.18.a 3.1. in preparation for, & in support of an Infantry raiding party at G.6.c.4.0

The bombardment will take place on X.Y & Z days. At zero time on Z day a barrage will be opened round the point of entry. Lanes will be cut through the wire at G.12.a.30.95. just N. of road & G.18.a.2.1. in front of Salient during daylight on X & Y days by 18 pounders & Trench Mortars.

Time	Task	X day	Rate	Amm.
9.0pm	Bombardment "A" (Tracing A)	18pdr. bombard front line & enfilade comm'n trenches. 6" Hows. bombard strong points & trench junctions behind front line 4.5 Hows Bombard comm'n trenches. T.M's " Front Line.	Intense	600 30
9.10pm	Barrage "B" (Tracing B).	18pdr. lift to support line & comm'n trenches 6" How. lift to trench junctions further back 4.5. How. lift to comm'n trenches further back T.M's bombard flanks.	Intense	600 30.
9.20pm	Bombardment "A" (Tracing A)	18pdr. 6" How 4.5 How T.M's } Drop back to "A" 18pdrs. use shrapnel.	Intense	300 30
9.25pm		ALL STOP		

"Y" Day

Time	Task	Y day	Rate	Amm.
9.0pm	Bombardment "C" (Tracing C)	18pdr. 6" How 4.5 How T.M's } Same as A.	Intense	400 30.
9.10pm	Barrage D (Tracing D)	18pdr. 6" How 4.5 How T.M's } Same as B	Intense	400.
9.20pm	Bombardment C (Tracing C)	18pdr. 6" How 4.5 How T.M's } Drop back to C 18pdrs. use shrapnel.	Intense	300 30.
9.25pm		ALL STOP.		

"Z" day.

Time	Task		Rate	Amm
-0.10	Bombardment C (Tracing C)	18 pdr. bombard front line & enfilade communication trenches 6" Hows. bombard strong points & trench junctions behind front line 4.5 Hows. bombard comm'n trenches T.M's Bombard front line	Intense	400 30
0.0.	Barrage "B" (Tracing B).	Bombard support line & communication trenches. 6" Hows. bombard trench junctions 4.5 Hows. bombard trench junctions T.M's bombard flanks.	Intense	1000 60
0.0.	Barrage "D" (Tracing D)	18 pdr 6" Hows 4.5 Hows T.M's Lift from C to D		600 30
0.20	Barrage "D" (Tracing D).	18 pdr. 6" Hows. 4.5 Hows. T.M's. Reduce rate of fire to Sec. Fire 1 min. till stop is ordered.		

TOTAL 18 pdr. 4600
4.5 How 300
6" How

19.8.16.

(Sgd). R. WELLESLEY Brig. Gen. R.A.
Commdg. 21st. Divl Artillery.

110th Brigade.

21st Division.

L/8th BATTALION

LEICESTERSHIRE REGIMENT

SEPTEMBER 1916.

Army Form C. 2118.

8th Leicesters Vol 12

WAR DIARY
or
INTELLIGENCE SUMMARY
(Erase heading not required.)

Instructions regarding War Diaries and Intelligence Summaries are contained in F. S. Regs., Part II. and the Staff Manual respectively. Title Pages will be prepared in manuscript.

Place	Date	Hour	Summary of Events and Information	Remarks and references to Appendices
Trenches. ARRAS. Sectors (98-101)	1-9-16		The day passed off very quietly AAA ~~During~~ About 3 pm the enemy dropped 4 Trench Mortars of large calibre just behind Trench 100 AAA No damage was done AAA Our Stokes Guns replied with good effect. The night was noticeable for the large number of Very Lights that the enemy sent up. Heavy Transport was heard behind the enemy's lines about 11.45 pm.	
	2.9.16		During the morning our artillery fired on the enemy's support trenches, one shell blowing up a bomb store. At 2 pm the enemy bombarded our trenches with Trench Mortars of all calibres, some damage was done to Trench 99 AAA. We had no casualties. At 6 pm we were relieved by the Cheshires "Bantam" Battalion. On being relieved the Battalion marched to Duisans, where the night was spent	
	3.9.16		At 9 am the Battalion fell in to march to 'Rest Billets' at LIGNEREUIL, a distance of about 16 kilometres from DUISANS. Order of march A. B. C. D. Headqrs Coys. The route taken was AGNEZ-LES-DUISANS, MONTENESCOURT, AVESNES-LE-COMTE to LIGNEREUIL. At 12.30 pm the Battalion halted for dinner about 2 kilometres from AVESNES, starting again at 1.45 and ultimately arriving at LIGNEREUIL at 4 pm.	
	4.9.16		The day was spent in Interior Economy & Bathing. The whole Battalion bathed during the day at the Mill BERLENCOURT about H24C2.2 ref map 51C.	
	5.9.16		Early morning Drill parade under R.S.M. 6.30 am – 7.15 am. Physical Training, Bayonet Fighting, Rapid Loading & Platoon Drill 9.15 – 12 noon, under Coy arrangements. Each Platoon was instructed in how to fire the Lewis Gun, and during the day each man fired, the range being situated at	

(I 92 7.2)

2149 Wt. W14957/M90 750,000 1/16 J.B.C. & A. Forms/C.2118/12.

Instructions regarding War Diaries and Intelligence Summaries are contained in F. S. Regs., Part II. and the Staff Manual respectively. Title Pages will be prepared in manuscript.

WAR DIARY
or
INTELLIGENCE SUMMARY
(Erase heading not required.)

Army Form C. 2118.

Place	Date	Hour	Summary of Events and Information	Remarks and references to Appendices
LIGNEREUIL	6.9.16	-	Parades same as yesterday. Bayonet Fighting took place under the supervision of the Brigade Staff Instructor in Bayonet Fighting in Wood about 200 yards East of Orderly Room. In the afternoon the C.O. took each Company in turn in March Discipline, Artillery Formation and Extended Order Drill at I21C.8.4. Specialists were under their own instructors	
	7.9.16		The Battalion fell in at 9 am for a Battalion Route March Route Ref Map 51C LIGNEREUIL - AMBRINES, X Roads H12 b7.4, SUS-LEZ-BOIS - DENIER LIGNEREUIL. Order of March A Coy Advance Guard Hq Signallers B C & D Coys Lewis Gun Detachments in rear of Coys. The Battalion arrived back in billets 1.30 pm.	
	8.9.16		Early morning Parade as usual under R.S.M. AAA. Semaphore practice for officers under Signalling Officer 6.45 am to 7.30 am at I22a.0.5 AAA Practice in Rapid Wiring under Instructors of R.E.s AAA Bayonet Fighting and Rapid Loading under Coy arrangements. In the afternoon the Divl Bombing Officer gave a lecture to the Officers in Hq Mess.	
	9.9.16		Parades. Nonconformists 9 am. Church of England Brigade Parade Service 9.45 am. The Brigade Sports were held after Parade Service at I25 a.7.7. The Divl Band was in attendance, and the Divisional Concert party gave a performance. Dinners & Teas were served on the ground.	
	10.9.16		The Battalion paraded at 9.15 am for inspection by the G.O.C. the division. The inspection took place at I13 d.	

2149 Wt. W14957/M90 750,000 1/16 J.B.C. & A. Forms/C.2118/12.

Instructions regarding War Diaries and Intelligence Summaries are contained in F. S. Regs., Part II. and the Staff Manual respectively. Title Pages will be prepared in manuscript.

WAR DIARY
or
INTELLIGENCE SUMMARY
(Erase heading not required.)

Army Form C. 2118.

Place	Date	Hour	Summary of Events and Information	Remarks and references to Appendices
11-9-16. Lignereuil	–	–	Parades as usual. Specialists under their own instructors. In the afternoon from 2pm to 3pm the new draft were on parade under their CSM's AAA. From 2pm to 3pm the NCO's were under the RSM for instruction. The finals of the Inter-Battalion boxing matches took place in the evening.	
12.9.16	–	–	The day was spent in Interior Economy and preparation for departure on the 13th.	
13.9.16	–	–	The Battalion fell in at 10 am to march to FREVENT, where they were entraining for the SOMME AREA. AAA Dinners were partaken of on the way, and FREVENT was reached about 3.30 pm. AAA On arrival Teas were served out. The Battalion bivouaced in a field near to FREVENT Station until midnight when they entrained. DERNANCOURT the detraining station was reached about 2pm on the 14th.	
14.9.16			On ~~arrival~~ detraining at DERNANCOURT the Battalion marched 2 miles to the bivouacing area, where they bivouaced for the night.	
15.9.16.			The Battalion fell in, in order of march at 7am, and marched to DERNANCOURT where packs were dumped prior to going into action. At 1pm the march was continued until a point was reached between FRICOURT and MEAULTE, where the Battalion bivouaced for the night.	

2149 Wt. W14957/M90 750,000 1/16 J.B.C. & A. Forms/C.2118/12.

Army Form C. 2118.

Instructions regarding War Diaries and Intelligence Summaries are contained in F. S. Regs., Part II. and the Staff Manual respectively. Title Pages will be prepared in manuscript.

WAR DIARY
or
INTELLIGENCE SUMMARY

(Erase heading not required.)

Place	Date	Hour	Summary of Events and Information	Remarks and references to Appendices
16.9.16	–	–	These two days were spent in rest AAA	
17.9.16			About 8 pm on the 17th the Battalion ~~marched~~ fell in to march to a place about ½ mile east of TRONES WOOD AAA The route taken was through MAMETZ and MONTAUBAN. The place where the Battalion were going to bivouac was reached about 11 pm, the Transport stopping about 2 miles behind.	
17th – 24th.			During these days the Battalion was in reserve AAA Working parties and carrying parties were found for the troops who were holding the line and consolidating the positions they had won. While the Battalion were in bivouacs East of Trones Wood they had 7 casualties owing to the accidental exploding of a bomb.	
24 – 31			About 7 pm on the night on the 24th the Battalion marched up to take a position prior to making an attack the ~~[illegible]~~ next day. Before they reached the position the enemy heavily shelled our men, several casualties resulting. At 12.30 pm on the 25th the first attack was launched, the 5th Bn being in a position on the right of FLERS. The objective was the first German Line, a distance of about 1000 yards from the trench from which the Battalion launched the attack. The attack was made in "waves" each platoon forming a wave and 2 waves going "over" at a time. The attack was launched with splendid heroism the first objective	

Army Form C. 2118.

WAR DIARY
or
INTELLIGENCE SUMMARY
(Erase heading not required.)

Instructions regarding War Diaries and Intelligence Summaries are contained in F. S. Regs., Part II. and the Staff Manual respectively. Title Pages will be prepared in manuscript.

Place	Date	Hour	Summary of Events and Information	Remarks and references to Appendices
17–31st			was gained in about ¾ of an hour, The men then stopped a short time to consolidate their gain, and to allow the artillery barrage to lift AAA They then pressed on to their second objective which was the village of GUEUDECOURT. By the time they reached the village their ranks were sadly thinned by the tremendous artillery barrage the enemy put up, and by Machine guns which wrought terrible havoc. Nevertheless with dauntless gallantry they pressed on, reaching the village and engaging the enemy in hand to hand fighting, which took place all the night. In the morning the 7th Bn relieved the 8th Bn in the village, and the enemy were finally driven out. The 8th Bn were brought back to the second line of trenches, where they were relieved by the 6th Bn on the 28th. They then went back to Swiss Trench, where they remained until relieved on the night of Oct 1st	
			J. W. [illegible] J. T. [illegible] for Major Comdg 8th (Ser) Bn Leicestershire Regt	

2149 Wt. W14957/M90 750,000 1/16 J.B.C. & A. Forms/C.2118/12.

8th Leicesters

Instructions regarding War Diaries and Intelligence Summaries are contained in F. S. Regs., Part II. and the Staff Manual respectively. Title Pages will be prepared in manuscript.

WAR DIARY
or
INTELLIGENCE SUMMARY
(Erase heading not required.)

Army Form C. 2118.

8th Leicester

Vol ~~12~~ 13

Place	Date	Hour	Summary of Events and Information	Remarks and references to Appendices
Bernafay Wood	1-10-16	–	The Battalion after coming out of action on the night of the 1st, bivouaced for the night on the outskirts of BERNAFAY. WOOD.	
DERNANCOURT	2-10-16		The Battalion fell in at 11am to march to DERNANCOURT AAA The latter place was reached at 4pm, dinners being served on arrival.	
	3-10-16		The day was spent in Interior Economy + General cleaning up AAA The men got their packs back from the Brigade Dump.	
	4-10-16		At 1-30 pm the Battalion paraded in full marching order to entrain at DERNANCOURT Station AAA. The station was reached at 3pm, and the process of entraining commenced AAA After being in the train about 7 hours LONGPRÉ the detraining station was reached. Before starting away from the station tea was served out. The Battalion then marched to PONT REMY a distance of about 7 miles, arriving there at 3am 5-10-16. Billets had previously been secured here.	
PONT. REMY.	5-10-16 6-10-16		These days were spent in Interior Economy, and Bathing.	
	7-10-16		At 10-30 pm the Battalion fell in to go to PONT REMY Station, prior to entraining for the 1st Army Area. A fatigue party had been at the station during the day engaged in loading the Transport AAA The entraining + loading was completed about midnight. BETHUNE the detraining station was reached at 10-30 pm. 8-10-16.	

2449 Wt. W14957/M90 750,000 1/16 J.B.C. & A. Forms/C.2118/12.

Army Form C. 2118.

Instructions regarding War Diaries and Intelligence Summaries are contained in F. S. Regs., Part II. and the Staff Manual respectively. Title Pages will be prepared in manuscript.

WAR DIARY
or
INTELLIGENCE SUMMARY

(Erase heading not required.)

Place	Date	Hour	Summary of Events and Information	Remarks and references to Appendices
	8-10-16.		After detraining at Bethune Station the Battalion marched to FOUQUEREUIL a distance of 2½ miles. AAA Here billets had been secured.	
FOUQUEREUIL	9-10-16		Rifle + Gas Helmet Inspection under Coy arrangements AAA Deficiencies in ammunition made up AAA Bathing parades under Coy arrangements.	
	10-10-16		The Battalion paraded in full marching order outside Hq mess, preparatory to taking over the Hohenzollern Sector of Trenches AAA The parade fell in in the following order D. C. B. A. Hq Coy. Lewis Gun Handcarts marched in the rear of the Battalion. They marched to the trenches via Fouquieres Bethune and Sailly La Bourse. The 8th Bn Leicestershire Regt relieved the 2nd Rifle Brigade in the Reserve Sector of Trenches the relief being completed about 3 pm.	
Hohenzollern Reserve Sector of Trenches	11-10-16		Our dispositions were as follows, B Coy on the left of Hq, and 'D' on the right. 'A' + 'C' Coys were billetted in the village of VERMELLES. Parades:- 9am to 10am Squad + Arm drill under Coy arrangements AAA During the time the Battalion were in the Reserve Sector permission was given for 25% of each Company to visit the "Divisional Concert Party" at SAILLY-LA-BOURSE.	
	12-10-16		Parades same as for the 11-10-16.	
	13-10-16		During the day all officers + Company Sergeant Majors visited the trenches that the Battalion were going to take over when they left the Reserve Sector	

2449 Wt. W14957/M90 750,000 1/16 J.B.C. & A. Forms/C.2118/12.

Instructions regarding War Diaries and Intelligence Summaries are contained in F. S. Regs., Part II. and the Staff Manual respectively. Title Pages will be prepared in manuscript.

WAR DIARY
or
INTELLIGENCE SUMMARY
(Erase heading not required.)

Army Form C. 2118.

Place	Date	Hour	Summary of Events and Information	Remarks and references to Appendices
HOHENZOLLERN Reserve Sector of Trenches	14.10.16		The Battalion was reinforced by a draft of 2 officers + 10 men AAA Parades:- as usual. The Baths ~~[illegible]~~ at VERMELLES were open for the benefit of the Battalion from 10am – 12 noon	
	15.10.16		During the time that the Battalion were in the Reserve trenches, working parties were found for the 7th Bn. who were in the front line	
	16.10.16		Nothing to report	
	17.10.16		The 8th Bn. Leicestershire Regt relieved the 7th Bn. in the front + reserve line trenches at 1.45 in the following order:- C+A Coys relieved C+A Coys of the 7th Bn. in the reserve line, C Coy relieving by way of GORDON ALLEY and A Coy HULLUCH ALLEY. B+D Coys of the 8th Bn relieved B+D of the 7th Bn in the front line trenches ¼ of an hour later. B Coy through HULLACH ALLEY and D Coy through GORDON ALLEY. The relief was complete at 3.10 pm.	
	18.10.16		The following alterations were made in the dispositions of the Coys in the Reserve & Front Lines AAA A+B Coys were relieved by ~~[illegible]~~ Coys of the 1st Lincoln Regiment A + B, then moved to the positions which were formally	

Army Form C. 2118.

WAR DIARY
or
INTELLIGENCE SUMMARY

(Erase heading not required.)

Instructions regarding War Diaries and Intelligence Summaries are contained in F. S. Regs., Part II. and the Staff Manual respectively. Title Pages will be prepared in manuscript.

Place	Date	Hour	Summary of Events and Information	Remarks and references to Appendices
	18.10.16		occupied by C+D Coys. In the meantime C+D Coys of the 8th Bn relieved 2 Coys of the 9th Bn up to NEW CUT. The reliefs were complete at 9.30 p.m.	
	19.10.16		Enemy artillery were fairly active during the afternoon, and at 5.30 p.m. dropped 8 105 mm H.E. Shells on Reserve Trench near GORDON STATION, causing slight damage to the trenches. During the night we sent out a patrol of 1 Officer, 1 NCO + 20 Rs to find out if it was possible to get in the rear of enemy's crater posts from Sap 108 with a view to carrying out a raid AAA The patrol found this to be impossible. The patrol ran foul of a German Sentry Group and were fired on with bombs + rifles AAA. No casualties resulted.	
	20.10.16		Enemy artillery were inactive during the day AAA. Between 2.30 p.m. + 4.30 p.m. our Artillery + Trench Mortars carried out a combined shoot on the enemy's reserve lines, and the shots appeared to have done considerable damage to the enemy's trenches. During the night a patrol was sent out for reconnaissance purposes. They discovered an enemy trench filled in by wire	
	21.10.16		In reply to our "shoot" of yesterday enemy sent over 50 Trench Mortars of various calibres chiefly on left of Posty and round left Boyau. Slight damage was done to the trenches but we had no casualties	

2149 Wt. W14957/M90 750,000 1/16 J.B.C. & A. Forms/C.2118/12.

Instructions regarding War Diaries and Intelligence Summaries are contained in F. S. Regs., Part II. and the Staff Manual respectively. Title Pages will be prepared in manuscript.

WAR. DIARY
or
INTELLIGENCE SUMMARY
(Erase heading not required.)

Army Form C. 2118.

Place	Date	Hour	Summary of Events and Information	Remarks and references to Appendices
SUPPORT TRENCHES	22.10.16.		A & C Coys of the 8th Bn were relieved by B & D Coys of the 7th Bn. + B & D Coys of the 8th by A & C of the 7th. A Coy relieved by way of Barts Alley to the Supports, and C Coy down Saville Row and Gordon Alley to the Supports. B & D Coys relieved by way of Barts Alley. The relief was complete at 10.45 am.	
	23.10.16		Our dispositions were as follows:- JUNCTION KEEP B Coy, CENTRAL KEEP C Coy, Railway Reserve Trench between Quarry Ally + Central Keep D Coy, RAILWAY KEEP A Coy. One platoon of each Coy garrisoned the Keep, while the remainder of the men were in the front line of the respective Keeps.	
	24.10.16.		The Brigade Baths at VERMELLES were at the disposal of the Battalion from 2pm to 6pm. AAA During the time the Battalion are in the Support Trenches 10% of the NCOs + men are allowed to go to the Divisional Cinema at SAILLY-LA-BOURSE each day.	
	25.10.16		Working Parties + Carrying Parties were found for the 6th Bn. 1 officer + 20 men were detailed to dig out SAVILLE ROW at its junction with V150 St AAA 1 officer + 20 men to wire Reserve trench Northwards from Left Boyau.	

2449 Wt. W14957/M90 750,000 1/16 J.B.C. & A. Forms/C.2118/12.

Army Form C. 2118.

Instructions regarding War Diaries and Intelligence Summaries are contained in F. S. Regs., Part II. and the Staff Manual respectively. Title Pages will be prepared in manuscript.

WAR DIARY
or
INTELLIGENCE SUMMARY

(Erase heading not required.)

Place	Date	Hour	Summary of Events and Information	Remarks and references to Appendices
SUPPORT TRENCHES	26.10.16		The G.O.C. granted about 180 men of the Battn, who had completed two years service, Good Conduct badges. The Brigade Baths at VERMELLES, were at the disposal of the Battalion AAA During the evening about 40 NCO's and men availed themselves of the opportunity of going to the Cinema at SAILLY-LA-BOURSE, buses conveying the party from Philosophe Corner, VERMELLES	
	27.10.16		During the day an officer and company sergeant-major from each company, took over the Trench Stores from the 7th Bn, prior to the Battalion going into the line on the next day	
	28.10.16		The 8th Bn relieved the 7th Bn in the Front Line and Immediate Support Line Trenches during the morning. The relief was complete at 11.am. The day was very quiet with the exception that between 5 pm + 5.30 pm, the enemy fired 13 shells which fell behind VIGO St.	
	29.10.16		Our artillery were fairly active during the day and appeared to have done damage to the enemy's front line trenches AAA. A searchlight was repeatedly shone on our lines and caused a certain amount of annoyance to one of our wiring parties. During the night heavy Transport was heard from the direction of HULLUCH.	

Army Form C. 2118.

Instructions regarding War Diaries and Intelligence Summaries are contained in F. S. Regs., Part II. and the Staff Manual respectively. Title Pages will be prepared in manuscript.

WAR DIARY
or
INTELLIGENCE SUMMARY

(Erase heading not required.)

Place	Date	Hour	Summary of Events and Information	Remarks and references to Appendices
Hohenzollern Sector of Trenches	30-10-16		The day was fairly quiet but during the morning the enemy dropped 4 Medium sized Trench Mortars which fell in DRUMMOND TRENCH, and Knocker in the Trenches. Our Trench Mortars replied effectively silencing those of the enemy. The night was noticeable for the amount of Machine Gun Fire on both sides. The enemy appeared to be very nervous, and during the night sent up a good many very lights. We had a patrol out, which was used as a screen to one of our wiring parties which was at work.	
	31-10-16		Another quiet day. At 12.20am our artillery opened fire on G.4.d 60.65. Eight rounds were fired, but it was impossible to observe the shots. At 9pm a patrol went out for reconnaissance purposes, and returned safely about 10.30pm.	

J.W. Dean Smith
Lt & Adjt. for Lt-Col.
Cmdg 8th (Ser) Bn Leicestershire Rgt.

2449 Wt. W14957/M90 750,000 1/16 J.B.C. & A. Forms/C.2118/12.

8th Leicestershire Regt

(1)

Vol 14

Instructions regarding War Diaries and Intelligence Summaries are contained in F. S. Regs., Part II. and the Staff Manual respectively. Title Pages will be prepared in manuscript.

WAR DIARY
or
INTELLIGENCE SUMMARY
(Erase heading not required.)

Army Form C. 2118.

Place	Date	Hour	Summary of Events and Information	Remarks and references to Appendices
Hohenzollern Sector of Trenches	1-11-16		Our artillery were fairly active during the afternoon, and at 2.30pm the 18 pounders fired 20 rounds at G4.d.b.2.95. At 4.15pm enemy sent over several Trench Mortars in retaliation to our artillery fire. These fell near dump in rear of NORTHAMPTON TRENCH, and caused slight damage to the Trench AAA. During the night we sent out a patrol of 1 officer, 1 N.C.O. and 2 privates for the purpose of reconnoitring NO MANS LAND. Some useful information was gained relating to the condition of the enemy's wire. At 1.15pm the enemy blew a mine 30 yards short of Post 2 (Sand 6.6) and at 1.25pm three Germans were seen to dash round lip to highest point of crater & then vanish out of sight AAA Some damage was done to our trenches, but we had no casualties	
	2-11-16.		The day passed off rather quietly. During the night a searchlight situated further North played right along our sector AAA Another patrol was sent out during the night being out for about 2 hours. They spotted a German wiring party of about 12 men, and on returning to our lines shortly afterwards informed the Lewis Gunners, who fired on this party, with good effect as it is evident from the noise that was heard, that one or more of the party were hit.	
	3-11-16		The Battn was relieved in the front line Trench, and the "Immediate Supports" by the 7th Leicesters the relief being completed at 10.45 am	

Instructions regarding War Diaries and Intelligence Summaries are contained in F. S. Regs., Part II. and the Staff Manual respectively. Title Pages will be prepared in manuscript.

WAR DIARY
or
INTELLIGENCE SUMMARY
(Erase heading not required.)

Army Form C. 2118.

(2)

Place	Date	Hour	Summary of Events and Information	Remarks and references to Appendices
Hohenzollern Sector of Trenches (Reserve)	4-11-16.		Holy Communion was held at 9.30 am in Advanced Dressing Station 65th Field Ambulance AAA Parade Service at 11 am in the Cinema Hut, SAILLY-LA-BOURSE AAA This was in the nature of a farewell service as the Chaplain, Capt Woollcombe is leaving the Battalion for duties elsewhere.	
	5-11-16		During the time the Battalion was in the Reserve Sector of trenches, permission was given for 25% of the NCO's and men to visit ~~the~~ BETHUNE or the neighbouring village, also for 8 men per Coy. to visit the Divisional Concert Party at SAILLY-LA-BOURSE	
	6-11-16.		Carrying Parties were found for the Trench Mortar Battery, and Working Parties for the R.E's AAA Free beer was provided for the NCO's and men at the Canteens.	
	7-11-16		Working Parties same as for yesterday AAA The Brigade Baths at VERMELLES were at the disposal of the Battalion from 2 pm to 6 pm.	
	8-11-16.		During the day the officers, NCO's and men were fitted with the new Box Respirator at the Gas Chamber, Vermelles AAA 4 NCO's from Divisional Hdqrs and Cpl Lawrence of the 8th Battalion supervised the 'fitting on' of these helmets	

2449 Wt. W14957/M90 750,000 1/16 J.B.C. & A. Forms/C.2118/12.

Army Form C. 2118.

(8)

Instructions regarding War Diaries and Intelligence Summaries are contained in F. S. Regs., Part II. and the Staff Manual respectively. Title Pages will be prepared in manuscript.

WAR DIARY
or
INTELLIGENCE SUMMARY
(Erase heading not required.)

Place	Date	Hour	Summary of Events and Information	Remarks and references to Appendices
RESERVE Sector of Trenches Hohenzollern	9-11-16		The 8th (Ser) Bn Leicestershire Regiment relieved the 7th (Ser) Bn Leicestershire Regiment in the Front Line trenches, and Immediate Supports. Our dispositions were. C Coy Left Coy front Line, + A Coy Right Coy front line. D + B Coys were in support to C + A Coys respectively. During the night enemy machine guns were very active, continually sweeping our parapets AAA Our Lewis Gun fired intermittently in retaliation. We had no patrols out owing to the bright moon	
FRONT LINE Sector of Trenches	10/11/16		Enemy Trench Mortars were fairly active during the whole of the day, and between 2.45 pm and 4.45 pm they fired 15 Heavy trench Mortars on to NORTHAMPTON TRENCH Owing to the very bad state of the trenches in the front line, our men were employed in clearing falls etc The Germans appear to be in the same "boat" as during the day numerous Germans were seen on the top of the trenches. Our Snipers claim 2 hits	
	11-11-16		Our artillery were very active during the day, and our 4.5's fired on the enemy's Support trenches with what appeared to be good effect AAA. Our Stokes Guns were also very active and during the day fired 70 rounds on the enemy front line AAA The enemy retaliated with an ~~Arial~~ Aerial Dart display 20 darts falling in NORTHAMTON TRENCH and LEFT BOYAU. No damage was done.	

2449 Wt. W14957/M90 750,000 1/16 J.B.C. & A. Forms/C.2118/12.

Instructions regarding War Diaries and Intelligence Summaries are contained in F. S. Regs., Part II. and the Staff Manual respectively. Title Pages will be prepared in manuscript.

WAR DIARY
or
INTELLIGENCE SUMMARY

(Erase heading not required.)

Army Form C. 2118.

(4)

Place	Date	Hour	Summary of Events and Information	Remarks and references to Appendices
Hohenzollern Salient Trenches Front Line	12-11-16		There was the usual amount of Trench Mortar activity on both sides AAA About 3 pm our artillery were active shelling the villages behind the German lines AAA The Germans opposite our sector seem to have tried to adopt a friendly attitude and there are indications that a relief has recently taken place.	
	13-11-16		The day was unusually quiet AAA The Germans were persistently seen walking on the top of their trenches presumably the reason being the bad state in which their trenches must be. Our snipers claimed several hits.	
	14-11-16		At 11 am 3 Heavy Trench Mortars fell behind junction of SAVILLE ROW and NORTHAMPTON TRENCH but without doing any damage AAA Between 2pm + 4pm 25 Aerial Darts were fired into SAVILLE ROW AAA At 12 noon our Stokes Guns fired 30 rounds into the enemy's front line in retaliation the shots seems to do a considerable amount of damage to the enemy's trenches. A patrol went out from NEW CUT at 9 pm for reconnaissance purposes. The enemy appeared to be very nervous and sent up numerous Very Lights, which appeared to come from the ~~[illegible]~~ Support Line. Enemy machine guns hampered the patrol.	
	15/11/16		The Battalion was relieved by the 7th (Ser) Btn Inniskilling Regt in the front line + Immediate Supports AAA After being relieved the Battalion went into the Support line the dispositions being A+D Coys in Central Keep, B Coy in Junction Keep and C Coy in Railway Keep	

2249 Wt. W14957/M90 750,000 1/16 J.B.C. & A. Forms/C.2118/12.

Army Form C. 2118.

(6)

Instructions regarding War Diaries and Intelligence Summaries are contained in F. S. Regs., Part II. and the Staff Manual respectively. Title Pages will be prepared in manuscript.

WAR DIARY
or
INTELLIGENCE SUMMARY

(Erase heading not required.)

Place	Date	Hour	Summary of Events and Information	Remarks and references to Appendices
SUPPORT LINE Hohenzollern Sector	16/11/16		The Brigade Baths were at the disposal of the Battalion from 2 pm to 6 pm AAA Working parties were found for the Trench Mortar Battery. During the first three days in the Support Line, two men per Coy, were allowed to proceed to Bethune.	
	17/11/16		The following working parties were found by the Battalion. 1 Officer + 25 ORs ~~to report to~~ reported to Support Coy Hq at junction of CENTRAL BOYAU – RESERVE TRENCH at 6 pm. Two parties each of 1 Officer + 15 ORs, one reported at RESERVE TRENCH at Right Coy Hdqrs, the other at Company Hdqrs in BACK ST.	
	18-11-16 19-11-16 20-11-16		Usual working found for Bns in front line, and RE's. AAA The Brigade Baths were at the disposal of the Bn on the 20th.	
	21-11-16		The Battalion relieved the 7th Bn in the front line trenches, and Immediate Supports. Relief complete at 11.15 am.	
	22-11-16		Our Trench Mortars were active from 10.30 am, ~~and~~ to 12 noon, firing on enemy's front line. AAA During the afternoon enemy fired several trench Mortars on our front line, but without doing any damage. During the night several enemy working parties were heard AAA A Lewis Gun was taken out between Posts 10 + 11. As the gun was preparing for action a loud cough was heard from the enemy's lines, and their working party disappeared	

Instructions regarding War Diaries and Intelligence Summaries are contained in F. S. Regs., Part II. and the Staff Manual respectively. Title Pages will be prepared in manuscript.

WAR DIARY
or
INTELLIGENCE SUMMARY
(Erase heading not required.)

Army Form C. 2118.

(5)

Place	Date	Hour	Summary of Events and Information	Remarks and references to Appendices
Front Line Hohenzollern Sector of Trenches.	23/11/16		Between 11am and 12 noon the enemy sent over about 20 aerial darts, which fell on and around CORK ST AAA These slightly damaged the trench AAA. Between 1.30 pm + 3.30 pm our artillery carried out a combined shoot with our Trench Mortars on enemy front + support lines opposite both sectors. About 90 rounds were fired by our 18 pounders + heavies, and seemed to do a considerable amount of damage to the enemy trenches.	
	24/11/16		From 8am to 11am the enemy carried out an organised "strafe" with mortars of all sizes AAA Considerable damage was done to our trenches the sap at the top of LINCOLN ST being blown in. Retaliation was asked for by the Right Sector, but the spasmodic efforts of our 18 pdrs and Stokes Mortars seemed quite unable to make any impression AAA At 10am a medium T.M. fell close to junction of VIGO ST and SAVILLE ROW, killing one man and wounded 5 others. The enemy seemed to have been searching for our T.M.s round DRUMMOND TRENCH and SAVILLE ROW.	
	25/11/16		Enemy Trench Mortars were active between 11am and 3pm, and 95 medium trench mortars were fired on our front line ~~between~~ around NORTHAMPTON TRENCH AAA Slight damage was done to our trenches. Between 1pm + 3pm our 18 pdrs fired 100 rounds in retaliation to enemy trench mortar fire. Considerable damage was done to the enemy's trenches. A patrol went out from our lines during the night for reconnaissance purposes.	
	26/11/16		During the day the enemy fired many 10.5 cm shells on our line but did no damage. They were also very active with aerial darts. Our Stokes guns retaliated between 12 noon + 1pm, on the enemy front line opposite Vigo St.	

Instructions regarding War Diaries and Intelligence Summaries are contained in F. S. Regs., Part II. and the Staff Manual respectively. Title Pages will be prepared in manuscript.

WAR DIARY
or
INTELLIGENCE SUMMARY
(Erase heading not required.)

7

Army Form C. 2118.

Place	Date	Hour	Summary of Events and Information	Remarks and references to Appendices
Hohenzollern Sector of Trenches. ~~Support~~ Support Line	27/11/16		The Bn. were relieved in the front line trenches & Immediate Supports by the 7th Bn. Our disposition were B & C Coys in the village of MAZINGARBE ~~and~~ A Coy in VERMELLES and D Coy in LANCASHIRE TRENCH AAA During the ~~stay~~ time in Reserve, 25% of the N.C.O's + men, were allowed to visit BETHUNE and the neighbouring villages.	
	28/11/16 29-11-16 30-11-16		The Brigade Baths at VERMELLES were at the disposal of the Battalion ~~of the Battalion~~ during these 3 days. Working parties were found for the Battalions in the front line, and the usual working parties found for the Trench Mortars + R.Es.	
	~~30-11-16~~			

R.H.R. Dawson.
2nd Lt + A/Adjt for Lt Col.
Cmdg 8th (Ser) Bn. Leicestershire Regiment

2449 Wt. W14957/M90 750,000 1/16 J.B.C. & A. Forms/C.2118/12.

Instructions regarding War Diaries and Intelligence Summaries are contained in F. S. Regs., Part II. and the Staff Manual respectively. Title pages will be prepared in manuscript.

WAR DIARY
or
INTELLIGENCE SUMMARY.
(Erase heading not required.)

8th Leicester R. (1)

Army Form C. 2118.

Vol 15

Place	Date	Hour	Summary of Events and Information	Remarks and references to Appendices
Hohenzollern Sector of Trenches Reserve Line	1/12/16.		The Brigade baths were at the disposal of the Battalion from 2 pm to 6 pm AAA	
	2/12/16		The usual working + carrying parties were found for the RE's, Trench Mortar Battery, and the Battalions in the front line.	
	3/12/16.		The Battalion relieved the 7th Bn. Leicestershire Regiment in the front line trenches AAA Details of relief annexed.	
Front Line Hohenzollern Sector of Trenches			The enemy's Trench Mortars were active between 9am + 11am, medium Trench Mortars falling round junction of BARTS ALLEY + NORTHAMPTON TRENCH AAA No damage was done. Our Trench Mortars fired about 30 rounds on enemy's front line in retaliation. At 3.10 pm 3 green Very lights were fired by enemy opposite No 7 Post. No action followed. Our working parties were chiefly engaged in cleaning the trenches	
	4/12/16		Enemy Trench Mortars were very active during the day chiefly between 11am + 1pm AAA 23 Medium T.M.s fell in and around CORK ST. but did no damage to the trenches AAA Our Mortars retaliated between the hours of 12 noon + 3 pm, and from the amount of débris thrown up, seemed to be causing a considerable	

2353 Wt. W2544/1454 700,000 5/15 D. D. & L. A.D.S.S./Forms/C. 2118.

Instructions regarding War Diaries and Intelligence Summaries are contained in F. S. Regs., Part II. and the Staff Manual respectively. Title pages will be prepared in manuscript.

WAR DIARY
or
INTELLIGENCE SUMMARY.
(Erase heading not required.)

(2)

Army Form C. 2118.

Place	Date	Hour	Summary of Events and Information	Remarks and references to Appendices
Front Line Hohenzollern Sector	4/12/16		amount of damage to the enemy trenches.	
			A patrol of 2 NCO's and 6 men left Lincoln St at 1am. for reconnaissance purposes AAA This patrol located a sentry group opposite LINCOLN ST, and found the enemys wire to be very strong.	
	5/12/16		At 11am the enemy fired 4 77cm shells about 50 yards in rear of OB4 AAA His Trench Mortars were also active, mostly falling round junction of LINCOLN ST and VIGO ST AAA Our Trench Mortars replied effectively.	
			Our Lewis Guns were instrumental in dispersing several enemy working parties, and from cries + noises which were heard, it is evident that the enemy had several casualties.	
			A hostile sniper opposite the head of LINCOLN ST. killed one of our sentries, and wounded another. The sniper post has been located and measures are being taken for the suppression of this sniper.	
	6/12/16		Enemy artillery ~~were~~ was active between 12 noon + 1pm, 15 4.2" shells falling in rear	

2353 Wt. W2544/1454 700,000 5/15 D. D. & L. A.D.S.S. Forms/C. 2118.

Instructions regarding War Diaries and Intelligence Summaries are contained in F. S. Regs., Part II. and the Staff Manual respectively. Title pages will be prepared in manuscript.

WAR DIARY
or
INTELLIGENCE SUMMARY.
(Erase heading not required.)

Army Form C. 2118.

(3)

Place	Date	Hour	Summary of Events and Information	Remarks and references to Appendices
Front Line Hohenzollern Sector	6/12/16		of DRUMMOND TRENCH AAA In retaliation our 18 pdrs shelled enemy front and support lines opposite N°90 + CRATER SECTORS and appeared to fire with good effect. A patrol of 1 NCO + 7 men left G4d. 95.25 at 1am in order to obtain identification and general information. The patrol encountered a strong enemy patrol, who hurriedly retreated to their trenches on the approach of our patrol. Useful information was gained with regard to the enemy wire which was in a very delapidated state, having apparently been scattered by our Trench Mortars.	
	7/12/16.		Annexed work report of the Bn. from 1/12/16 to 8/12/16. Enemy Artillery and Trench Mortars were inactive during the greater part of the day. Our Trench Mortars fired about 60 rounds on enemy front line opposite Sap 8 B. Results appeared to be very good. Hostile working parties were dispersed by our Lewis Gun Fire during the night.	
	8/12/16		Between 2 pm + 4 pm 15 c.m. shells fell in rear of junction of PANK + VIGO ST.	

2353 Wt. W2544/1454 700,000 5/15 D. D. & L. A.D.S.S. Forms/C. 2118.

Instructions regarding War Diaries and Intelligence Summaries are contained in F. S. Regs., Part II. and the Staff Manual respectively. Title pages will be prepared in manuscript.

WAR DIARY
or
INTELLIGENCE SUMMARY.
(Erase heading not required.)

(4)

Army Form C. 2118.

Place	Date	Hour	Summary of Events and Information	Remarks and references to Appendices
Hohenzollern Sector of Trench Front Line			causing slight damage AAA Between 9.15 am + 9.45 am 7 medium Trench Mortars	
	8/12/16		fell in and around NORTHAMPTON TRENCH, Considerable damage was done to the trench, but we had no casualties AAA. Our artillery and Trench Mortars were inactive.	
			We had no patrol out during the night, owing to the light night.	
	9/12/16		The 8th Bn. were relieved in the Front Line + Immediate Supports by the 7th Bn. Leicestershire Regt AAA	
			Details of relief annexed.	
			Dispositions A Coy Railway Reserve Trench.	
			B Coy Junction Keep.	
			C Coy Lancashire Trench (N of Reserve Btn HQ)	
			D Coy Central Keep.	
	10/12/16		Working + Carrying Parties were found for REs + T.M. Battery AAA	
			Church Services were held in the Brewery Vermelles + an evening Service in the Cinema, Sailly. The Brigade Baths were at the disposal of the Bn. from 2 pm to 6 pm	

Army Form C. 2118.

Instructions regarding War Diaries and Intelligence Summaries are contained in F. S. Regs., Part II. and the Staff Manual respectively. Title pages will be prepared in manuscript.

WAR DIARY
or
INTELLIGENCE SUMMARY.

(Erase heading not required.)

Place	Date	Hour	Summary of Events and Information	Remarks and references to Appendices
~~Reserve~~ Support Trenches Hohenzollern Sector	11th – 14th Dec		Usual Working + Carrying Parties found for Battalion in front line, and the RE's. On Dec 13th the Battalion was reinforced by a draft of 90. OR.	
	15th Dec		The Bn was relieved in the Support Lines by the 9th Bn Kings Own Yorkshire Light Infantry AAA Details of relief annexed. When the relief was complete the Bn marched to BETHUNE where billets had previously been arranged in the CANDLE FACTORY.	
BETHUNE	16th Dec		All kit was thoroughly inspected under Company arrangements. Baths were allotted to the Battalion from 8 pm to 3 pm. The CO inspected the new draft in the yard of the CANDEE FACTORY at 2.30 pm.	
DO	17th Dec		Church Parade was held in the Theatre. The Battalion marched to the theatre by Companies in succession, A Coy leading AAA A parade for	

2353 Wt. W2544/1454 700,000 5/15 D. D. & L. A.D.S.S. Forms/C. 2118.

Instructions regarding War Diaries and Intelligence Summaries are contained in F. S. Regs., Part II. and the Staff Manual respectively. Title pages will be prepared in manuscript.

WAR DIARY
or
INTELLIGENCE SUMMARY.
(Erase heading not required.)

(6)

Army Form C. 2118.

Place	Date	Hour	Summary of Events and Information	Remarks and references to Appendices
BETHUNE	17 Dec		Nonconformists was held in the YMCA at 10am AAA. There was a service for Roman Catholics in the church of ST VAAST at 10.30am.	
	18th Dec		Parades took place under Company arrangements from 9am to 11am on the Parade Ground VERQUIN RD (reference map FRANCE Sheet 36B NE Edition 6 E23d.6.9)	
	19th Dec		Parades under Company Arrangements as per yesterday. Company for Duty A Coy. Orderly Officer 2nd Lt Bennett.	
	20th Dec		The Battalion moved to AUCHEL in the Reserve Division Area. Details of move annexed. On arrival at Auchel the Battalion marched to billets which had been arranged by 2nd Lt Davis and the 4 CQMSs.	
AUCHEL	21st Dec		Parades Arm Drill + Platoon Drill under Coy arrangements from 10am to 11.30am. The Medical Officer gave a lecture to Stretcher Bearers in the	

(7)

Army Form C. 2118.

WAR DIARY
or
INTELLIGENCE SUMMARY.
(Erase heading not required.)

Instructions regarding War Diaries and Intelligence Summaries are contained in F. S. Regs., Part II. and the Staff Manual respectively. Title pages will be prepared in manuscript.

Place	Date	Hour	Summary of Events and Information	Remarks and references to Appendices
AUCHEL	21st		Regimental Aid Post at 10·45 am.	
DO	22nd		The Baths were at the disposal of the Battalion during the day AAA Parades ~~in the a~~ from 10 am to 11·30 am took place under Company arrangements Company for duty A Coy. Orderly Officer 2nd Lt Rawley.	
DO	23.		Parades The Battalion paraded on the Royal Flying Corps ground S.E of the AUCHEL-LOZINGHEM Road. Companies marched to the parade ground independently, the parade being under Coy arrangements. The CO lectured to all Officers at 2·30 pm.	
DO	24		The following C of E services were held in the Evangelical Temple Holy Communion 8 am Voluntary Service 11·30 am Evening do 5 pm A Parade Service for Nonconformists was held in the Evangelical Church at 9 am	

2353 Wt. W2544/1454 700,000 5/15 D. D. & L. A.D.S.S. Forms/C. 2118.

Army Form C. 2118.

WAR DIARY
or
INTELLIGENCE SUMMARY.
(Erase heading not required.)

(8)

Instructions regarding War Diaries and Intelligence Summaries are contained in F. S. Regs., Part II. and the Staff Manual respectively. Title pages will be prepared in manuscript.

Place	Date	Hour	Summary of Events and Information	Remarks and references to Appendices
AUCHEL	25th		CHURCH PARADE A C of E. Service was held in the Evangelical Temple at 9 am. Companies marched independently to the Church. A Parade Service was held for Nonconformists in the Protestant Evangelical Church Xmas dinners were served at 1.30 pm AAA A C + D Coys had their dinners in the Schools. B Coy having their dinner in their billet. The Officers + Senior NCO's waited on the men who seemed to thoroughly enjoy themselves	
DO	26.		During the afternoon a football match, Officers v Sergeants was played on the Royal Flying Corps ground, the result being Officers 3 goals, Sergeants 4 goals. The Divisional Concert Party gave a concert to the Brigade in the Gymnasium AUCHEL commencing at 6 pm.	
DO	27		Parades under Company Arrangements AAA The Divisional Band played in ~~the~~ AUCHEL as follows, 10 am to 11 am to 8th Bn. 11.15 am to 12.15 pm to 6th Bn.	

Instructions regarding War Diaries and Intelligence Summaries are contained in F. S. Regs., Part II. and the Staff Manual respectively. Title pages will be prepared in manuscript.

WAR DIARY
or
INTELLIGENCE SUMMARY.
(*Erase heading not required.*)

Army Form C. 2118.

(9)

Place	Date	Hour	Summary of Events and Information	Remarks and references to Appendices
AUCHEL	28/12/16		Parades under Coy arrangements AAA During the afternoon the "Lena Ashwell" Concert Party gave a Séance in the Gymnasium.	
do	29/12/16		Lieut Col Beaman 64th Field Ambulance gave a lecture "on his experiences whilst a prisoner in Germany" to the 6th + 8th Bns in the Gymnasium The Divisional Band played in AUCHEL from 10am to 11am. Parades from 9.30am to 11.30am on the Royal Flying Corps Ground under Coy arrangements.	
do	30/12/16		Baths were allotted to the Battalions from 9am to 1pm. In the afternoon the C.O. gave a lecture to the Bn in the Divisional Theatre on the "Importance of Sentry Duties".	
do	31/12/16		Church Services were held as follows:- Church of England In the Divisional Theatre, Rue de Temple, Parade Service at 10am.	

Instructions regarding War Diaries and Intelligence Summaries are contained in F. S. Regs., Part II. and the Staff Manual respectively. Title pages will be prepared in manuscript.

WAR DIARY
or
INTELLIGENCE SUMMARY.
(Erase heading not required.)

(10) Army Form C. 2118.

Place	Date	Hour	Summary of Events and Information	Remarks and references to Appendices
AUCHEL.	31/12/16.		ROMAN CATHOLIC Parade Service at 9.30am in the Church AUCHEL NONCONFORMIST Parade Service at 8.45am in the Evangelical Church, Rue de Temple. The Divisional Band played the "Old Year" out and the "New Year" in, on the Square AUCHEL. TLWarner Major Cmdg. 8th (Ser) Bn Leicestershire Rgt.	

2353 Wt. W2544/1454 700,000 5/15 D. D. & L. A.D.S.S. Forms/C. 2118.

File / Copy No. 11

SECRET.

OPERATION ORDERS BY
MAJOR T. L. WARNER, COMMDG.,
6TH. (SER) BN. LEICESTERSHIRE REGT. 2-12-16.

---

1. **RELIEF.** The Battalion will ~~be~~ relieve ~~d~~ the 7th. Battn. Leicestershire Regt. in the Front Line tomorrow, the 3rd.inst.

2. **DISTRIBUTION.**
A & D Companies will be in the Front Line, B & C Coys in support.

3. **ROUTES.** A Coy. will go to VIGO SECTOR marching by HULLUCH ALLEY, GORDON ALLEY and SAVILLE ROW and will enter HULLUCH ALLEY at 6-30a.m.

B. Coy. will go to RESERVE TRENCH by HULLUCH ALLEY and GORDON ALLEY entering HULLUCH ALLEY at 6-45a.m.

C. Coy. will move to RESERVE TRENCH, LEFT SECTOR by BARTS ALLEY entering BARTS ALLEY at 6-45a.m.

D. Coy. will move to CRATER SECTOR by BARTS ALLEY, RESERVE TRENCH and SAVILLE ROW entering BARTS ALLEY at 6-15a.m.

B. & C. Coys. will leave MAZINGARBE at 7-30a.m. marching by ½ Coys. at 200 yards distance, B. Coy. leading.

4. Each Coy. will send an Officer & a senior N.C.O. to take over at Coy. H. Q. of the 7th. Battn. at 6-30a.m.
The same N.C.O. will hand over at the time of next relief.

5. Handing and Taking Over Forms will be in Battn. Hdqrs. by 12noon, 3rd. inst.

6. 1 Officer from C. Coy. and 1 N.C.O. & 3 men from both B. & C. Coys. will remain behind at MAZINGARBE to clean up billets and will not move off until O.C. B. & C Coys. of the 7th. Battn. are satisfied with the condition of the billets.
The 2 N.C.O's of these parties will meet an Officer and 2 N.C.O's of the 7th. Battn. at MAZINGARBE CHURCH at 7a.m. and will show them the billets.

7. Relief complete will be wired by the code:-

"NO R. E. WORKING."

8. **SPARE KIT.** Coys. spare kit will be dumped as follows:-
A. & D. Coys. at CLARKES KEEP at 7-30a.m.
B. & C. Coys. at the School, MAZINGARBE at 7a.m.
1 N.C.O. and 3 men from A. Coy. will beleft in charge at CLARKE'S KEEP.
1 N.C.O. and 3 men from C. Coy. will be left in charge at MAZINGARBE.
These parties will not move off until the kit has been removed by the Transport.
Men's spare kit will consist only of 1 or 2 blankets, spare tunic and trousers.
Washing Kit, ordinary boots, puttees, and Gum boots will be taken into the trenches.

9. **TRANSPORT.** A limber for each Coy. will be at MAZINGARBE at 7a.m. to take men's gum boots and Blankets, and Officers kit, mess kit and cooking utensils etc. to CLARKE'S KEEP.
B. Coys. limber will be at the Mission.
C. " will be at the School.
Each man must tie his boots and blankets together.
Kit must be loaded in order of platoons and unloaded in the reverse order.

(Charles ...)

2/Lt. & A/Adjt.
6th. (Ser) Bn. Leicestershire Regt.

PTO

Distribution

Copy No 1 'A' Coy
" 2 'B' "
" 3 'C' "
" 4 'D' "
" 5 C.O.
" 6 Medical Officer
" 7 Transport "
" 8 Quartermaster
" 9 R.S.M.
" 10 7th Bn Leicestershire Regt
" 11 File

Work Report of the

8th. (Ser) Battn. Leicestershire Regt.

from Noon 1-12-16 toNoon 8-12-16.

A. **Craters and Saps.**

In CRATER Sector No.5 & 6 Posts, were cleaned, ~~and~~ deepened and strengthened. The Sap at head of LINCOLN STREET was cleared out and deepened.

B. **Front Line.**

Two new bays were made (1) in VIGO ST. by Coy. H.Q. (2) at bottom of PANK ST.

Dog's leg Blocks were built in LINCOLN ST. (2) in PANK ST.

CORK ST. was cleared where it had been blown in.

2 New shelters were built in VIGO ST.

NORTHAMPTON TRENCH was cleared after various falls and deepened South of Coy. H. Q.

In RESERVE TRENCH two bays were rebuilt between GORDON ALLEY and SAVILLE ROW. N. of BARTS ALLEY firebays were rebuilt and revetted; and sumps cleared and deepened.

A flying traverse was built in front of the canteen.

C. **SUPPORT LINE.** N I L.

D. **RESERVE LINE.** N I L.

E. **COMMUNICATION TRENCHES.**

One flying traverse in BARTS ALLEY was strengthened another was erected.

F. **WIRING.**

Wiring was done continuously in front of LINCOLN ST. and the wire in front og Posts 1 and Posts 5 and 6 was strengthened.

G. **DUGOUTS** under 98th. Field Coy. R.E.

Carrying was done for this Coy. on 2-12-16.

Beds were erected in dugouts in NORTHAMPTON TRENCH and VIGO ST.

H. Schemes of 170th. (T) Coy. R. E. N I L.

(sd) R.M.R.Davison 2/Lt &
A/Adjt.

8-12-16.

SECRET.

OPERATION ORDERS BY
LT. COL. H.L. BEARDSLEY, COMMDG.,
8TH. (SER) BATTN. LEICESTERSHIRE REGT. 8-12-16.

---

1. **RELIEF.** The Battn. will be relieved in the Front Line by the 7th. Battn. Leicestershire Regt. at about 9-30a.m. tomorrow 9th. inst.

2. **ROUTES.** On reliefs Coys. will march as follows:-
A. Coy. to that part of RAILWAY RESERVE TRENCH immediate South of QUARRY ALLEY, via SAVILLE ROW, RESERVE TRENCH, HARTS ALLEY and CENTRAL KEEP.

B. Coy. to JUNCTION KEEP via SAVILLE ROW and GORDON ALLEY.

C. Coy. to that part of LANCASHIRE TRENCH which lies North of RESERVE BATTN. H. Q. via GORDON ALLEY, NEW CUT and HARTS ALLEY.

D. Coy. to CENTRAL KEEP via SAVILLE ROW and HARTSXALLEY.

Cooking utensils, Officers kit and mess Kit will start immediately after Breakfast.

3. **TAKING OVER.** An Officer and a senior N.C.O. from each Coy. will report at 8-45a.m. to O.C. Coys. of the 6th. Batn. Leicestershire Regt. in SUPPORT LINE for the purposes of taking over. The same N.C.O's will hand over on next relief.

4. All dugouts, shelters etc. will be vacated by 9a.m. and will only be occupied thereafter in exceptional circumstances and with the permission of O.C. Coys.

5. One Officer per Coy. will be left in charge of a party consisting of 1 N.C.O. & 8 men who will go round all dugouts etc. and ensure that they are left clean. This party will not leave the sector until the O.C. Coy. 7th. Battn. Leicestershire Regt. is satisfied with the condition of the dugouts, shelters etc.

6. Handing over and Taking over forms will be in Hd. Qrs. by 12 noon.

7. Relief complete will be wired by code:-
"1000 ROUNDS."

8. O.C. Coys. will ensure that all ranks remove their gumboots and put on dry socks as soon as possible after ~~xx~~ arrival in SUPPORT LINE.

9. While in SUPPORT LINE passes to BETHUNE and the neighbouring villages may be given daily to 10% of each Coy.

[illegible]

2/Lt. & A/Adjt.
8th. (Ser) Bn. Leicestershire Regt.

DISTRIBUTION.

Copy. No.	1	C. O.	Copy No.	2	Adjt.
	3	R.S.M.		4	A. Coy.
	5	B. Coy.		6	C. Coy.
	7.	D. Coy.		8	7th. Leicesters.
	9.	Qtr. Mtr.		10	File.

SECRET.

OPERATION ORDERS BY
LT. COL. H. L. BEARDSLEY, COMMDG.
8TH. (SER) BATTN. LEICESTERSHIRE REGT.

Copy No.

14-10-16.

---

1. RELIEF. The Battalion will be relieved in the Support Line by the 9th. Battn. King's Own Yorkshire Light Infantry at about 9a.m. on the 15th. inst.

2. GUIDES. Each Coy. will send 1 guide per platoon to be at CLARKES KEEP at 8-30a.m. These guides will each be provided with a slip stating the position of his platoon for the information of the incoming platoon.

Guides will lead incoming Coys. as follows:-

Guides from B. Coy. will bring up B. Coy. of the 9th. K.O.Y.L.I. by HULLUCH ALLEY.

Guides from A. Coy. will bring up D. Coy. of the 9th. K.O.Y.L.I. by QUARRY ALLEY.

Guides from D. Coy. will bring up C. Coy. of he 9th. K.O.Y.L.I. by BARTS ALLEY.

Guides from C. Coy. will bring up A. Coy. of the 9th. K.O.Y.L.I. by VERMELLES ROAD.

Guides from H. Q. Coy. will bring up H. Q. Coy. of the 9th. K.O.Y.L.I. by BARTS ALLEY.

3. ROUTES. As soon as the last platoon of each relieving Coy. reaches a sector, the Coy. relieved in that sector will march off by platoons at 200 yards distance - Lewis Gun leading.

Companies will march as follows:-

A. Coy. by LEFT BOYAU and QUARRY ALLEY.
B. Coy. by GORDON and BARTS ALLEY.
C. Coy. by the VERMELLES ROAD.
D. Coy. by the trench leading over the railway to Battn. H.Q. and by BARTS ALLEY.
H. Q. Coy. by BARTS ALLEY.

4. ORDER OF MARCH. Companies will march in order of relief by platoons at 200 yards distance along the VERMELLES - PHILOSOPHE ROAD to PHILOSOPHE CROSS ROADS, thence by the NOYELLES - SAILLY LABOURSE - BEUVRY ROAD to BETHUNE.

LEWIS GUN TEAMS will load up handcarts immediately on leaving the trenches and will follow in rear of their Coys. 200 yards distance from the last platoon.

5. HANDING OVER. All trench stores, log books, maps, aeroplane photographs, defence schemes etc. will be handed over and receipts obtained.

Very Pistols and Snipers rifles will not be handed over.

Coy. Commanders will be responsible that all dugouts shelters etc. are left scrupulously clean.

Handing over forms will be in H.Q. by 12 noon 16th. inst.

Completion of relief will be reported by code "25th. inst."

6. COOKS' UTENSILS. All Coys. dixies and cooking utensils will be at CLARKES KEEP at 7a.m. where they will be put on 2 limbers and taken to SAILLY LABOURSE by the route specified in para. 4 of these orders.

The Cooks will accompany these limbers and will report immediately on arrival to the Qtr. Mtr.

7. OFFICERS' KITS etc. Officers' Kits and Mess Kits will be at CLARKES KEEP at 8-30a.m. where they will be put on to the Mess Cart and G. S. Wagons at 10-30a.m.

The Medical Officer will also arrange for all R.A.P. material to be at CLARKES KEEP at 8-30a.m. where it will be put on to the Maltese Cart.

OPERATION ORDERS (Contd)

8. LOADING PARTIES. 1 N.C.O. and 4 men per Coy. under a Sgt. from C. Coy. will be at CLARKES KEEP at 8-15a.m. for the purpose of loading KITS etc. dumped there. They will accompany the Transport when loaded going by the route indicated.

1 N.C.O. and 3 men from each Coy. will be at 9-15a.m. at the open space off the main BETHUNE ROAD, N.W. of PHILOSOPHE to load mens' blankets and packs on transport detailed for that purpose.

9. PACKS etc. As each platoon arrives at the open space mentioned in para. 8 of these orders packs and blankets will be dumped - each platoon separately - and the platoon will then continue its march to BETHUNE. Blankets will be rolled and strapped to packs, and each pack must be clearly marked with the mans' name and number.

Packs and blankets will be loaded on limbers and lorries at 10-45a.m. under the TRANSPORT OFFICER.

Limbers will laod 1st. and the loading party will accompany the lorries when the packs etc. of the last platoon of the Battn. have been loaded but no man will under any circumstances ride on a loaded limber.

10. PLATOON DISTANCES. West of SAILLY LABOURSE the distance of 200 yards between platoons need not be adhered to.

11. BILLETS. On arrival in BETHUNE platoons will be marched straight to the billet in the CIGAR FACTORY.

12. DRAFT. The new draft will march to BETHUNE under LT. J.W.DIXIE SMITH leaving SAILLY LABOURSE at 8-30a.m.

Packs and blankets will be left at the transport lines and will be loaded on to the Motor Lorries after they have left PHILOSOPHE.

This party will also march straight to the billet.

13. DINNERS. Dinners will be served when the arrival of each Coy. is completed.

14. TAKING OVER. 2/LT. A.J.FLETCHER and the 4 Q.M.Sgts. will report at 7-30a.m. to the Hdqrs. of the 1ST. EAST YORKSHIRE REGT. in BETHUNE at the CHATEAU opposite the CIGAR FACTORY and will take over the billets.

[signature]
2/Lt. & A/Adjt.
8th. (Ser) Bn. Leicestershire Regt.

DISTRIBUTION.

Copy No.	1	C.O.	Copy No. 2	M.O.
	3	Q.M.&T.O.	4	A. Coy.
	5.	B. Coy.	6	C. Coy.
	7	D. Coy.	8	R.S.M.
	9	9th. K.O.Y.L.I.	10	File.

09

SECRET.

OPERATION ORDERS BY
LT.COL. H.D.BEARDSLEY, COMNDG.,
8TH. (SER) BN. LEICESTERSHIRE REGT 19-12-16

Ref. Map. BELGIUM Sheet 5A. 1/100,000.

1. MOVE. The Battalion will move tomorrow 20th. inst. to AUCHEL in the RESERVE DIVISION AREA.

2. ROUTE. The route followed will be by CHOCQUES to PONT DU REVEILLON, thence by ALLOUAGNE and LOZINGHEM to AUCHEL.

3. ORDER OF MARCH.

The Battalion will ~~pa made~~ parade in full marching order ready to march off at 9-30a.m.

Coys. will line up facing the CIGAR FACTORY in the following order A. B. C. D. & Hd. Qrs. Coy. The right of A. Coy. will rest on t he Junction of the RUE DE LILLE and the RUE MICHELET. Hd . Qrs. Coy. will parade on the left. LEWIS GUN TEAMS will march in rear of their Coys. Cookers and Transport will be in rear of the Battalion.

4. OFFICERS' KITS.

Officers' Kits will b e dumped by 8-30a.m. inside the WEST GATE of the FACTORY and will be loaded on to G.S. WAGONS. Officers' Servant s will be responsible that these kits are loaded.

5. MESS KITS.

Officers' Mess Kits will be ready at 8-30a.m. and will be called for by the Mess Cart in the following order of Coys.

A. C. B. D.

6. BLANKETS.

Mens' Blankets will be carried in 2 Lorries. They will be packed in Bundles of 10, each bundle clearly marked by Coys. and stacked inside the WEST GATE of the FACTORY by 8-30a.m.

7. LOADING PARTY.

1 N.C.O. (full rank from A. Coy.) and 10 men (2 per Coy. including H. Q. Coy.) wil l be at the WEST GATE at 8-15a.m. to supervise the stacking of the blankets. This party will load blankets on to the lorries and travel with them as baggage guard.

8. MEDICAL STORES.

The Maltese Cart will report to the M. O. at the Aid Post at 8-30a.m.

9. DINNERS.

Dinners will be served on arrival in AUCHEL.

(sd) R.M.R.Davison, 2/Lt. & A/Adjt.
8th .(Ser) Bn. Leicestershire Regt.

Instructions regarding War Diaries and Intelligence Summaries are contained in F. S. Regs., Part II. and the Staff Manual respectively. Title pages will be prepared in manuscript.

WAR DIARY
or
INTELLIGENCE SUMMARY.
(Erase heading not required.)

8th Leicester Regt.

Army Form C. 2118.

Vol 16

Place	Date	Hour	Summary of Events and Information	Remarks and references to Appendices
AUCHEL.	1/1/17 to 26/1/17		During the period stated, the Battalion was in rest at AUCHEL. A Training Programme was carried out an example of which is attached. Brigade Sports consisting of Boxing, Cross Country Running & Football, Bayonet Fighting, Rapid Wiring etc took place. While in rest at AUCHEL the Battalion were reinforced by a draft of 100 OR. Lt Col. G C I Hervey rejoined the Battalion, and assumed command 5/1/17.	
	29/1/17		The Battalion entrained at LILLERS, at 8 pm to move to the 2nd Army area, detraining at PROVEN about midnight. From here the Battalion marched to WINNEZEELE, a distance of about 10 kilometres, and were billetted in the district.	
WINNEZEELE.	29/1/17 to 31/1/17		Training was carried out, route marching being one of the principal features. While in training most severe weather was experienced.	

RM Dawson
2nd Lt & Adjt for Lt Col. Cmdg
8th (Ser) Bn Leicestershire Regt.

2353 Wt. W2514/1454 700,000 5/15 D. D. & L. A.D.S.S./Forms/C. 2118.

8TH (SER.) BN. LEICESTERSHIRE REGT.

PROGRAMME OF WORK FOR WEEK ENDING 27TH. JANUARY, 1917.

DATE	COY	TIME	WORK PROPOSED
22-1-17	A	9 to 9.30	Physical Training
		9.30 to 10.15	1 Platoon, Rapid Wiring
			2 do. Bayonet Fighting
			1 do. Bombing
		10.15 to 12.30	Musketry
	B & C	9 to 9.30	Physical Training
		9.30 to 10.30	Musketry
		10.30 tp 11	Bayonet Fighting
		11 to 11.30	Gas Drill -
		11.30 to 12	Platoon and Company Drill
	D	8.30 to 10.30	Musketry
		10.30 to 11.15	Physical Training
		11.15 to 12	1 Platoon, Rapid Wiring
			2 do. Bayonet Fighting
			1 do. Bombing
	ALL COYS	2 to 3p.m.	Saluting Drill, Arm Drill, Platoon Lectures.
23-1-17	A & D	9 to 9.30	Physical Training
		9.30 to 10.30	Musketry
		10.30 to 11	Bayonet Fighting
		11 to 11.30	Gas Drill
		11.30 to 12	Platoon and Company Drill
	C	8.30 to 10.30	Musketry
		10.30 to 11.15	Bayonet Fighting
		11.15 to 12	1 Platoon, Bombing
			2 do. Physical Training
			1 do. Rapid Wiring
	B	9 to 9.30	Bayonet Fighting
		9.30 to 10.15	1 Platoon, Bombing
			2 do. Physical Training
			1 do. Rapid Wiring
		10.15 to 12.30	Musketry
	ALL COYS	2 to 3p.m.	Saluting Drill, Arm Drill, Tactical Exercises.
24-1-17	A	8.30 to 10.30	Musketry
		10.30 to 11.15	Wood Fighting
		11.15 to 12	1 Platoon, Rapid Wiring
			2 do. Bayonet Fighting
			1 do. Bombing
	B & C	9 to 9.30	Bayonet Fighting
		9.30 to 10.30	Musketry
		10.30 to 11.15	Gas Drill
		11.15 to 12	Platoon and Company Drill
	D	8.30 to 9.15	1 Platoon, Rapid Wiring
		~~9.15 to~~	2 do. Bayonet Fighting
			1 do Bombing
		9.15 - 10.15	Wood Fighting
		10.15 12.30	Musketry

PROGRAMME OF WORK. (Contd.)

DATE	COY.	TIME	WORK PROPOSED
25-1-17	B	8-30 to 10-30	Musketry
		10-40 to 11-20	Wood Fighting
		11-25 to 12noon.	1 Platoon, Rapid Wiring
			2 Platoons, Physical Trng.
			1 Platoon, Bombing
	A & D	9 to 9-30	Bayonet Fighting
		9-35 to 10-30	Musketry
		10-40 to 11-10	Gas Drill
		11-15 to 12	Platoon and Coy. Drill
	C	8-30 to 9-15	1 Platoon, Bombing
			2 Platoons, Physical Trng.
			1 Platoon, Rapid Wiring
		9-20 to 10-10	Wood Fighting.
		10-15 to 12-30	Musketry
	ALL COYS.	2 to 3p.m.	Saluting and Arm Drill, Tactical Training.(under Coy. arrangements.)
26-1-17	A	9 to 10a.m	Baths
	B	10 to 11	Baths
	C	11 to 12	Baths
	D	12 to 1p.m.	Baths
			Raiders will bathe with C. Coy. Hdqrs. Details and Transport with their Coys.
			Parades under Coy. arrangements.
	ALL COYS.	6p.m.	Marking out Trenches
27-1-17	ALL COYS.	9 to 12-30	Route march and Foot Inspection.
	ALL COYS.	2-30 to 3p.m.	Saluting and Guard Drill under Coy. arrangements.

2/Lt. & Adjt.
8th. (Ser) Bn. Leicestershire Regt.

110th INFANTRY BRIGADE.

The following COMPETITIONS ETC. will be held during the period the Brigade is in the Back Area. Full details of each event will be furnished later.

I. **ASSOCIATION FOOTBALL.** Inter-Company. "Knock-out". 1st and 2nd Prizes.

II. **CROSS COUNTRY RUN.** Battn. team race. Teams of 30, distance about 3½ miles. Run in boots. Unlimited entry. 1st and 2nd Team Prizes. First ten men in receive prizes. In addition there will be a sealed number (a high one) entitling man to ten days leave. Must finish within 35 mins. of starting.

III. **BOXING.** Full details later.

IV. **SHOOTING.** Inter-Company Tile. Teams of 8 and leader (who does not shoot). Two Prizes.

V. **EVELYN WOOD.** (Inter-Battn.) Teams of 1 Officer and 40 men, all to belong to one Company. March 5 miles and shoot on completion of march. Dress - Full marching order. Marks for turn out, condition of team at end of march, number of hits. March to be completed in 80 minutes. Two Prizes.

VI. **WIRING.** Inter-Company, teams of 1 N.C.O. and 8 men. Drill will be issued later. 3 prizes.

VII, **BAYONET TRAINING.** Inter-Company Teams of 8. Three prizes.

VIII. **SNIPING.** Inter-Battn. team of 4 men. Distance 300 yds, small Fig. 3 target exposed for 3 seconds. Two prizes.

IX. **PHYSICAL TRAINING.** Inter-Company, teams of 20. Three prizes.

X. **BOMB THROWING.** Inter-Company, two men per Company. Three prizes.

XI. **STRETCHER BEARING.** Inter-Company, four men per Company. Three prizes.

XII. **SIGNALLING.** Inter-Battn. teams of 6. Two prizes. Bde. H.Q. count as a Battalion.

XIII. **MACHINE GUN.** Teams of 6. Two Prizes.

XIV. **LEWIS GUN.** Inter-Company, team of 6. Two prizes.

XV. **STOKES MORTAR.** Two Prizes.

P.T.O.

- continued -

XVI.	TRANSPORT.	Best pair of mules with harness. Best pair of H.D. with harness. Best single L.D. or cob with harness or pack saddlery. Best turn out - any vehicle, pair or single mule race, (if Course can be found).
XVII.	<u>TUG OF WAR</u>.	Inter-Battalion, catch weight. Teams of 10, best of three pulls.

In Competitions Nos. I, II, IX & XVII, the Machine Gun Company and Trench Mortar Battery will count as one Company if the O's. C. concerned so desire.

Entries for above will be asked for at an early date, and competitions will commence immediately.

------- o O o -------

4/1/17.

8th Leicester Rgt. Army Form C. 2118.

WAR DIARY
or
INTELLIGENCE SUMMARY.
(Erase heading not required.)

Instructions regarding War Diaries and Intelligence Summaries are contained in F. S. Regs., Part II. and the Staff Manual respectively. Title pages will be prepared in manuscript.

8th Bn Leicestershire Regt

Vol 17

Place	Date	Hour	Summary of Events and Information	Remarks and references to Appendices
WINNEZEELE	1/2/17 to 12/2/17		During this period training was carried out, route marching and tactical manoeuvres in the open being the principal features.	
	13.2.17		The Bn. moved into the 1st Corps Area, arriving at BETHUNE about 12 o'clock noon & billeting there until the next morning.	
	14.2.17		At 2 o'clock the Bn. marched to SAILLY LABOURSE & billeted there for the night.	
	15.2.17 to 21.2.17		The Bn. relieved the 1st. King's Shropshire Light Infantry in the trenches on the morning of the 15th & remained in the Front Line until relieved by the 7th (S) Bn. Leicestershire Regt on the 21st.	
	22.2.17 to 28.2.17		The Bn. went into Reserve at NOYELLES until the morning of the 27th when the 7th (S) Bn. Leicestershire Regt were relieved by them. On the 28th the Bn. took over the sector from the 1st Bn Lincolnshire Regt on the right of the sector they had been holding.	

[illegible] Lt. Col
Commdg 8th (S) Bn Leicestershire Regt.

6959.

SECRET. OPERATION ORDERS NO. 51. COPY No.
BY LT. COL. G.C.I.HERVEY, COMMDG.,
8TH. (SER) BATTN. LEICESTERSHIRE REGT.

Ref. Map. HAZEBROUCK 5A.

1. MOVE. The Battalion will move to the 1st. Corps Area on Tuesday 13th. inst.

2. ROUTE. The route followed will be by DROGLANDT - WATOU - due north to the MONARTBEEK - thence N.E. to PROVEN.

3. ORDER OF MARCH. The Battalion will be drawn up at 5-15a.m. in column of route facing South in the following order:-
S.W.Party, A. B. Hdqrs. Drums. C. D.
The head of the column will be just North of the Cross Roads 300 yards SOUTH of B. Coys. billets.

Horses for O.C. Coys. will be at the rendezvous.

4. KITS. Officers Kits and Mess Kits will be ready by 4-30a.m. dumped as follows:-
A. B. D. & Hdqrs. outside their respective billets.
C. Coy. outside S.W.Party Billet.

1 Lewis Gunner from each Coy. will be detailed to guard these kits until called for by Transport.

5. BLANKETS. Blankets will be dumped by 3-30a.m. outside Coy. billets with the exception of C. Coy's. which will be dumped outside S.W.Party Billet. Each platoons will arrange to have two dumps - one for the first blanket of each man - the other for the second blanket of all who have them. The "Second" Blankets will be loaded first. All blanket s will be rolled in bundles of 10 clearly marked with Coy. & Platoon.
One blanket per man will be drawn at PROVEN and carried in the train.
One lorry will call for Blankets of B & C Coys. and the S.W.Party and will carry guard 1 N.C.O. from B. Coy. and 2 men from each of B & C. Coys. and 1 man from S.W.Party.
One lorry will call for Blankets of A & D. Coys and Hdqrs and will carry as guard 1 N.C.O. from A. Coy. and 2 men from each of A & D. Coys. and 1 Signaller from Hdqrs.
These N.C.Os will be A/C.Q.M.S.

6. DETAILS. The 4 Lewis Gunners a nd Hdqrs. Mess waiter left as guard over each Coys. Officers' Kits and Mess Kits will report to the Transport Officer as soon as these kits are loaded.
Two Cooks per Coy. will remain with each Coys. Cooker.
Cooking Utensils of S.W.Party will be loaded on blanket lorry.
O.C. C & D. Coys. will detail one man to report to the Transport Officer at 6a.m. to accompany G.S. Limbered Wagons.

7. BAND. The Packs and Surplus equipment of the Band will be carried on the blanket lorries allotted to their respective Companies.

R.W.[illegible]
Lt. & Adjt.
8th.(Ser) Bn. Leicestershire Regt.

DISTRIBUTION.

Copy No. 1	C.O.	Copy No. 2	2nd. in Command.
3	T.O. & Q.M.	4	Med. Officer.
5.	A. Coy.	6.	B. Coy.
7.	C. Coy.	8.	D. Coy.
9.	O.C. S.W.Party.	10	R.S.M.
11	D[illegible]	12	File.

12-3-17.

SECRET.

OPERATION ORDERS NO. 52 Copy No.

BY LT. COL. G-C-I-HERVEY, COMMDG.,

8TH. (SER) BATTN. LEICESTERSHIRE REGT.

---

1. **MOVE.** The Battalion will move today 14th. inst. to the New Billeting Area at SAILLY LABOURSE.

2. **ROUTE** The Route followed will be by the BETHUNE - BEUVRY - SAILLY LABOURSE Road.

3. **ORDER OF MARCH.** The Battalion will be drawn up in column of route in the Rue MICHELET, ready to ma-rch off at 2-15p.m. in the followings order:-

   S.W.P. B. C. Drums. D. A. Hdqrs. Transport.

   The Head of the column will be at the Road Junction RUE DE LILLE - RUE MICHELET.

4. **OFFICERS MESS KITS.** Officers Mess Kits will be dumped at the Orphanage by 1-30p.m.

O.C. Coys. will ensure that Billets are left perfectly clean.

2/Lt. & Adjt.

8th. (Ser)Bn. Leicestershire Regt.

SECRET. OPERATION ORDERS NO. 53. Copy No.
BY LT. COL. G.C.I.HERVEY, COMNDG.,
8TH. (SER) BATTN. LEICESTERSHIRE REGT.

1. RELIEF. The Battalion will relieve the 1st. King's Shropshire Light Infantry, in the Front Line tomorrow 15th. inst.

2. ORDER OF MARCH. Coys. will march independantly by platoons at 200 yards distance, via PHILOSOPHE Cross Roads in the following order:-

D. Coy. 1st. Platoon to leave at 7-30a.m.
C. Coy.
A. Coy.
B. Coy.
S.W.Party
Headquarters.

3. LEWIS GUN LIMBERS. Lewis Gun Limbers will travel with the first platoon of each Coy, and will be at the cross Roads SAILLY LABOURSE at 7-30a.m.

4. GUIDES. Guides for each platoon will be at Clarke's Keep at 9a.m.

5. BLANKETS. Blankets will be clearly marked by Platoons rolled in bundles of ten and left outside Coy. Hdqrs. in charge of C.Q.M.S. and Drummers who will be responsible for taking them to the Q.M. Stores. S.W. Party and Hdqrs. outside respective men's billet.

6. MESS KITS. Officers Mess Kits and Trench Kits will be ready at 7a.m. dumped outside Coy. Hdqrs.

7. DIXIES. Dixies of each Coy. will be outside Coy. Hdqrs. at 7a.m. Dixies of Hdqrs. and S.W.P. will be ready at the same time outside their respective billets.

8. TRANSPORT. Each Coy. Hdqrs. & S.W.Party will send one guide to be at the Transport Lines at 6-45a.m. to guide limbers to Coy. Hdqrs. for the purpose of collecting Kits, Dixies etc.

9. TAKING OVER. O.C. Coys. will each send one Officer and a Senior N.C.O. half an hour before the Coy. marches off to take over trench stores etc.
Lists will be in Hdqrs. by 8p.m. 15th. inst.
The R.S.M. will take over for Hdqrs.

10. RELIEF COMPLETE. Relief complete will be wired by the following code word:-

A. Coy.	STYX.
B. and S.W.P.	ACHERON.
C. Coy.	LETHE.
D. Coy.	PHLEGETHON.

R W Emerson

Lt. & Adjt.
8th. (Ser) Bn. Leicestershire Regt.

File

O/o

SECRET OPERATION ORDERS NO. 54 Copy No. 12
BY LT.COL. G.C.I.HERVEY COMMDG.,
8TH.(SER) BATTN. LEICESTERSHIRE REGT.

20/2/17.

1. **RELIEF.** The Battalion will be relieved by the 7th. Battn. Leicestershire Regt. in the Front Line tomorrow 21st. inst., at about 9a.m.

2. **ROUTES.** Owing to HULLUCH ALLEY being impassable it will not be used at all tomorrow below GORDON DUMP.

B Coy of the 7th Battn. start at 7a.m. to relieve C Coy via BARTS ALLEY, RESERVE TRENCH and GORDON ALLEY, and will meet guides from C Coy at the junction of RESERVE TRENCH and GORDON ALLEY at 8a.m.

C Coy will go out by O.B.4 and STANSFIELD ROAD to VERMELLES direct.

D Coy of the 7th Battn. start at 8.15a.m. to relieve A Coy via BARTS ALLEY, RESERVE TRENCH and SAVILLE ROW.

Guides from A Coy will be at the junction of RESERVE TRENCH and SAVILLE ROW at 9a.m.

A Coy will go out via SAVILLE ROW, RESERVE TRENCH, GORDON ALLEY, O.B.4 and STANSFIELD ROAD.

A Coy of the 7th Battn. will start at 8a.m. to relieve D Coy via BARTS ALLEY, RESERVE TRENCH, GORDON ALLEY and HULLUCH ALLEY.

D Coy's guides will meet them at the junction of GORDON ALLEY and RESERVE TRENCH at 9a.m.

D Coy will go out via HULLUCH ALLEY, O.B.4 and STANSFIELD ROAD.

Great care must be taken to keep men down and conceal the relief, especially in RICHMOND TRENCH and HIGHLAND TRENCH and at the top of HULLUCH ALLEY.

Guides to these trenches will be instructed to warn incoming platoons to keep well concealed also.

C Coy of the 7th. Battn. will relieve B Coy, starting at 10.15a.m. via BARTS ALLEY and RESERVE TRENCH.

B Coy will go out when relieved via GORDON ALLEY, HULLUCH ALLEY, O.B.4 and STANSFIELD ROAD.

O.C.Coys will ensure that competent and reliable guides are sent to the Coy to be met and instructions given them in writing.

In going out good intervals are to be kept between platoons.

O.C. C Coy will post an intelligent sentry at the junction of O.B.4 and HULLUCH ALLEY to direct outgoing platoons down the southern portion of O.B.4 to STANSFIELD ROAD.

He will remain at this post until B.Coy has passed and will join the last platoon.

3. **OFFICER'S MESS KITS.** Officer's kits and Mess kits and Coy Cooking utensils etc., will leave Coy Hdqtrs. at 7a.m. Prompt via HULLUCH ALLEY, South end of O.B. 4 and STANSFIELD ROAD, and be carried to CLARKE'S KEEP and there be loaded on Mess Cart and limbers.

4. **ORDER OF MARCH.** On reaching CLARKE'S KEEP, Coys will march to NOYELLES by platoons at 200 yards distance.

5. **BILLETING.** Lt. J.W.Dixie Smith and the C.Q.M.Sgts will report at 9a.m. to the Hdqtrs. of the 6th.Battn. Leicestershire Regt. to take over billets.

6. **HANDING OVER.** An Officer of each Coy. of the 7th Battn. Leicestershire Regt. will report to the various Coy Hdqtrs. at 8a.m. to take over.

The Provost Sergt. will take over Hdqtrs. at the same time.

Handing Over Forms will be in Orderly Room by 2p.m. day of relief.

SHEET 2.

7. RELIEF COMPLETE. Relief Complet e will be wired by Code as follows:-

A Coy	ALICE
B "	WHERE
C "	ART
D "	THOU

transmitted by the O.C.Coy or other Officer who is the last to leave respective Coy Hdqtrs.

8. BLANKETS. Blankets will be dumped at CLARKE'S KEEP on arrival there by Hdqtrs and B Coy. an d will be rolled in bundles of 10, and loaded on the limbered G. S. Wagon provided for the purpose.

1 N.C.O.and 4 men of B Coy and 8 men of Hdqtrs. will remain with these blankets to load them and will accompany transport to NOYELLES.

9. GUM BOOTS. O.C.Coys are responsible that Gum Boots are taken off immediately on arrival in billets and dry socks put on, also that Gum Boots are washed and dried.

All Gum Boots and so cks for same will be collected at Coy Stores by 3p.m. and sorted in sizes. The Transport Officer will detail Transport to convey the 450 pairs of boots and socks to the Brigade Gum Boot Store after they have been collected.

10. SPECIAL WIRING PARTY. The S.W.P. will dump Gum Boots and Blankets at CLARKE'S KEEP at 9a.m. under a Lance Corporal and 1 O.R. These will be loaded on G.S. wagon and the S.W.P. will march direct to NOYELLES.

11. HORSES. O.C.Coys will find their horses at CLARKE'S KEEP.

[illegible]

Lt. and Adjt.
8th (Ser)Bn. Leicestershire Regt.

NOTE [illegible]

Distribution:- Copy No. 1 C.O.
2 2nd in Command
3 QM & T.O.
4 OC A Coy
5 " B "
6 " C "
7 " D "
8 R.C.S.M.
9 6th Leicestershire Regt.
10 7th " do
11 OC, S.W.P.
12 File

SECRET. OPERATION ORDERS NO.56 **COPY NO.** 12

BY LT. COL. G.C.I.HERVEY COMMDG.,

8TH (SER.) BATTN. LEICESTERSHIRE REGT. 27/2/17.

---

1. **RELIEF.** The 8th Battn. Leicestershire Regt. will relieve the 1st. Battn. Lincolnshire Regt. in the Front Line tomorrow 28th. inst.

2. **METHOD OF RELIEF.** One Coy. of the 9th. Bn. Leicestershire Regt. will relieve A. Coy. in VIGO SECTOR - relief to be complete by 9a.m.

A. Coy. will then relieve B. Coy. in RESERVE TRENCH.

On relief B. Coy. will proceed via GORDON ALLEY, O.B.1 and STANSFIELD ROAD to relieve the portion of the 1st. Battn. Lincolnshire Regt. holding the line from BOYAU 82 (Post 8.) to G.11.d.6.6. (Post 10.) inclusive.

Relief to be complete by 12 noon.

C. Coy. will relieve D. Coy. and take over HULLUCH and EAST CUT (i.e. A & B Posts.), starting at 8a.m. and completing relief by 9a.m. under Coy. arrangements.

On relief D. Coy. will take over from 1st. Bn. Lincolnshire Regt. Posts 10(a), 11, 12 and 13 moving via O.B.1 and STANSFIELD ROAD.

On relief by a Coy of the 6th. Battn. Leicestershire Regt. A Coy. will relieve a Coy of the 1st. Battn. Lincolnshire Regt. in O.G.1, STANSFIELD ROAD and HIGHLAND TRENCH moving by GORDON ALLEY and O.B. 1.

Hdqrs. Coy. will move at 11a.m. via GORDON ALLEY, O.B.4 and FOSSEWAY.

The S.W.Party will report to Hdqrs. HULLUCH ALLEY at 10.45a.m. and will move to their new quarters in O.B.2 with Hdqrs. Coy.

3. **GUIDES.** Guides for each platoon will be at the following points:-

At junction of O.G.1 and STANSFIELD ROAD for B Coy.

At junction of O.G.1 and FARMERS LANE for D Coy.

At junction of O.B.1.and STANSFIELD ROAD for A Coy.

At junction of O.B.4 and FOSSEWAY for Hdqrs. Coy.

4. **HANDING OVER.** One Officer and a Senior N.C.O. will be left to hand over , and all dugouts etc., will be left scrupulously clean.

5. **TAKING OVER.** One Officer and a Senior N.C.O. will take over in the new Sectors and will leave their present sectors one hour in advance of their Coys.

Handing and Takin g Over Forms will be in Hdqrs. (EXETER CASTLE) near junction of FOSSEWAY and O.B.1 by 2p.m.

Lt. and Adjt.

8th(Ser) Bn. Leicestershire Regt.

NOTE.

It is important that no hint of the relief of the next two days shall reach the enemy.

ALL troops must therefore keep to the trenches when carrying out reliefs and on no account must there be any going over the top.

DISTRIBUTION.

Copy No. 1	C.O.	Copy No. 2	2ndy in Command.
3	A Coy	4	B Coy
5	C "	6	D "
7	Q.M. and T.O.	8	R.S.M.
9	O.C.S.W.P.	10	PALM
11	ELM	12	File.

SECRET. OPERATION ORDERS NO 55. COPY NO. 12

BY LT. COL. G.C.I. HERVEY, COMMDG.,
8TH. (SER) BATTN. LEICESTERSHIRE REGT. 26-2-17.

1. **RELIEF.** The Battalion will relieve the 7th. Bn. Leicestershire Regt. in the Front Line tomorrow 27th. inst.

2. **ROUTES.** D. Coy. will proceed via HULLUCH ALLEY to Right Sector starting at 6-30a.m.

A. Coy. will proceed via HULLUCH ALLEY, GORDON ALLEY, RESERVE TRENCH, SAVILLE ROW to Left Sector starting at 6-40a.m.

C. Coy. will proceed via HULLUCH ALLEY, GORDON ALLEY, to Centre Sector starting at ~~6-46a.m.~~ 6.54 a.m.

B. Coy. will proceed via HULLUCH ALLEY to RESERVE TRENCH starting at 7-6a.m.

Hdqrs. Coy. will proceed via HULLUCH ALLEY starting at 7-18a.m.

Raiders and Employed Men will proceed to Billets at VERMELLES at 7-30a.m.

300 yards distance will be kept between platoons.

~~The Lewis Gun Team will accompany the first platoon of each Coy.~~

3. **KITS.** Officers Kits, Surplus Mess Kits and M.O's Panniers will be dumped at Aid Post before Coys. move off.
Men's spare kit and Blankets will be dumped at Coys. Hdqrs. before Coys. move off.
Transport will call for Kits at 7a.m. 6 Drummers will report to each C.Q.M.S. and Sgt. Drummer, to load at 7a.m.
A Limber and Maltese Cart will report at the Orderly Room at 6-30a.m. for Coy. Cooking Utensils, Orderly Room boxes etc.

4. **REPORT.** Coys. will report relief complete by:-

A.	Coy.	ABA
B.	"	ABOARD
C.	"	FOR
D.	"	DIXIE

5. **TAKING OVER.** 1 Officer and 1 Senior N.C.O. per Coy. will report to the respective Coy. Hdqrs. of the 7th. Battn. at 7a.m. and take over Stores etc.
The R.S.M. will take over for Hdqrs.
Taking Over Forms to be in Orderly Room by 3p.m. tomorrow 27th. inst.

6. **HANDING OVER.** 1 N.C.O. and 3 men per Coy. will remain behind under the Orderly Officer to hand over Huts etc. to the 7th. Battn. Huts will be left thoroughly clean.

2nd. Lt. Underwood.

Lt. & Adjt.
8th. (Ser) Bn. Leicestershire Regt.

DISTRIBUTION.

Copy No. 1	C.O.	Copy No. 2	2nd. in Command.
3	A. Coy.	4.	B. Coy.
5	C. Coy.	6	D. Coy.
7.	Q.M. & T.O.	8	Medical Officer
9.	7th. Bn. Leic. Regt.	10	R.S.M.
11.	Raiders & Hdqrs.	12	File

Instructions regarding War Diaries and Intelligence Summaries are contained in F. S. Regs., Part II. and the Staff Manual respectively. Title pages will be prepared in manuscript.

WAR DIARY
or
INTELLIGENCE SUMMARY.
(Erase heading not required.)

Army Form C. 2118.

8th Bn Leicestershire Regt.

Vol 18

Place	Date	Hour	Summary of Events and Information	Remarks and references to Appendices
	1.3.17 to 4.3.17		Trenches.	
	5.3.17 to 10.3.17		The Bn. was relieved by the 7th Bn. Leicestershire Regt. & stayed in "Supports" for 6 days	
	11.3.17 to 16.3.17		The Bn. relieved the 7th Bn. Leicestershire Regt in the Front Line. A successful raid on the German Line was carried out by a Raiding Party of the 110th Inf. Bde at 5 am. March 16th. 7 unwounded Germans were captured. 24 Germans were killed & wounded in their own Lines & 40 were reported killed in dug-outs. Our casualties were slight.	
	17.3.17 to 22.3.17		The Bn. was relieved by the 7th Bn. Leicestershire Regt. & proceeded to NOYELLES & remained there 6 days.	
	23.3.17 to 27.3.17		The 7th Bn. Leicestershire Regt. was relieved by this Bn. in the Front Line & it remained there until they were relieved by the 1st Bn. Leicestershire Regt. on the 27.3.17.	
	27.3.17 to 29.3.17		The Bn. remained in billets in MAZINGARBE until the morning of the 29th when	
	31.3.17		they proceeded by bus to New Area & billeted at LAHERLIÈRE.	

Guido C. Henry[?] Lt Col
Commdg 8th (S) Bn Leicestershire Regt.

2353 Wt. W2544/1454 700,000 5/15 D. D. & L. A.D.S.S./Forms/C. 2118.

Instructions regarding War Diaries and Intelligence Summaries are contained in F. S. Regs., Part II. and the Staff Manual respectively. Title pages will be prepared in manuscript.

WAR DIARY
or
INTELLIGENCE SUMMARY.
(Erase heading not required.)

Army Form C. 2118.

8th Bn Leicester Regt

Vol 19

Place	Date	Hour	Summary of Events and Information	Remarks and references to Appendices
			Reference Map - France. Sheet 51B S.W. Edition 4A	
La Herlière	1/4/17.		The Battalion ~~continued~~ remained in rest and continued to carry out Field Training.	
	2/4/17		The Battalion moved to ADINFER, where it bivouacked.	
	3/4/17.		The Bn. moved to HAMELINCOURT and bivouacked until the 5/4/17.	
	5/4/17		The Bn. moved forward and occupied the Outpost Line on the HENIN - CROISILLES Road. 'D' and 'C' Companies held the front line of posts in the sunken roads T.17.d & a. due north of CROISILLES 'B' Company were in support in the sunken road running through T.16.b, 17.a & c 'A' Coy. in reserve in the sunken road T.21.d. Bn. H.Q. in the Railway Embankment T.20.d.80.25. The Bn. held this line until the night of 12th/13th patrols were sent out continuously at night and contact was established with the enemy. Alteration in dispositions was made as follows - on the 9th Bn. H.Q. moved up to the sunken road in T.22.a.20.35. On the 11th 'A' Coy from reserve relieved 'D' Coy in the front line, as a consequence of heavy casualties suffered by 'D' Company, who lost 4 Officers and 15 O.R. on the night of 10/11th from enemy shell fire. 2nd Lieut. W.H. BENNETT was killed and 2nd Lieuts MESNY, DOUGLAS, and UNDERWOOD (died of wounds 16/4/17) being wounded.	
			On the morning of the 12th 'D' Coy under MAJOR T.L. WARNER carried out a minor enterprise in conjunction with the 6th Bn. ~~Leics~~ Regt. and the 64th INF. BDE. The operation was to bomb down the HINDENBURG TRENCH and take up a line close to and on three sides of FONTAINE-lez-CROISILLES.	

2353 Wt. W2314/1454 700,000 5/15 D. D. & L. A.D.S.S./Forms/C. 2118.

Instructions regarding War Diaries and Intelligence Summaries are contained in F. S. Regs., Part II. and the Staff Manual respectively. Title pages will be prepared in manuscript.

WAR DIARY
or
INTELLIGENCE SUMMARY.
(Erase heading not required.)

Army Form C. 2118.

Place	Date	Hour	Summary of Events and Information	Remarks and references to Appendices
			2	
			'D' Company continued the line of attack on the right of the 6th Bn. They were to keep in touch with the line of attack of the 64th BDE, but were to remain outside the wire of the HINDENBURG line. The operations were held up, very early in the day, owing to failure in the supply of bombs. MAJOR WARNER using every bit of cover afforded by the folds in the ground remained with 'D' Coy out in the open until midnight 12/13th, during which time the Coy. suffered casualties to 25 O.R.,	
	13/4/17		8 being killed. The same night, the Bn. was relieved by the 7th Bn. Leic. Regt. and marched to	
	14/4/17		bivouacs in MOYENVILLE, whence it moved to ADINFER bivouac on the 14th.	
BAILLEULMONT	15/4/17		The Bn. moved into billets at BAILLEULMONT, the division being in Corps Reserve. Training in Trench Tactics was carried out daily until the 23rd.	
	23/4/17		The division returning again to the line, the Bn. received orders to march at 1 hours notice to BOIRY St MARTIN, where it bivouacked until the 25th.	
	25/4/17		The BDE (110th) relieved the 100th BDE (33rd DIV) in the front line, the 8th Bn. being in support at St LEGER. The Bn. was not called upon to support the front line Bns. and suffered only three very slight casualties.	
	29/4/17		The Brigade moved into Divisional Reserve & the Bn. on being relieved by the 13th Bn. Northumberland Fusiliers moved to bivouacs at BOYELLES.	

Gerald C. Hervey Lt.Col.
Comdg 8th Leicestershire

2353 Wt. W2544/1454 700,000 5/15 D. D. & L. A.D.S.S./Forms/C. 2118.

21/110

Instructions regarding War Diaries and Intelligence Summaries are contained in F. S. Regs., Part II. and the Staff Manual respectively. Title pages will be prepared in manuscript.

WAR DIARY
or
INTELLIGENCE SUMMARY.
(Erase heading not required.)

8th Bn Leic Regt

Army Form C. 2118.

(3)

Reference - France. Sheet 51 B S.W.

8th Bn Leicester Regt

Vol 20

Place	Date	Hour	Summary of Events and Information	Remarks and references to Appendices
BOYELLES	1/5/17		The Battalion was bivouacked in S.18.b, north of the village. On the night of the 1st/2nd the 110th Inf. Bde. took over the positions of 64th Inf Bde. north of HINDENBURG Support Line, the 8th Bn Leic Regt forming the right assaulting battalion, was in BROWN TRENCH, T.6.a, N36c+d to road in O.31.C. The 9th Bn Leic Regt formed the left assaulting Bn, and held CURTAIN TRENCH from road in O.31.c to O.31.b.0.3. The 6th Bn Leic Regt was in support in N35a, and the 7th Bn Leics Regt in Reserve in N.34.b.	
	3/5/17		The attack on the village of FONTAINE-lez-CROISILLES was made on this day. There were three objectives, 1st SENSEE RIVER from approx. T.18.b.0.3 to U.2.b.5.5, 2nd Junction of SENSEE RIVER and SUNKEN ROAD at T.18.b.5.3 - U.7.c.6.5 - U.7.d.7.8 - thence round Eastern edge of FONTAINE to U.2.b.3.2. 3rd Army Boundary - U.13.c.7.3 - U.14.a.7.2 - U.14.c.4.3. The 64th Inf. Bde. to work South-Eastwards down HINDENBURG LINE. Two Tanks were attached to the 110th Inf. Bde.	
			Zero hour was at 3.45 a.m. (summer time), and the attack started under a creeping barrage. The Battalion was disposed in two waves of two lines each, with a wave of moppers up behind. From right to left 'A' Coy (Lt F.R. Oliver) 'B' Coy (Capt. A.G. ASTLE) 'C' Coy (MAJOR T.L. WARNER) formed the line of attack - each company having a two platoon frontage.	

Army Form C. 2118.

Instructions regarding War Diaries and Intelligence Summaries are contained in F. S. Regs., Part II, and the Staff Manual respectively. Title pages will be prepared in manuscript.

WAR DIARY
or
INTELLIGENCE SUMMARY.

(Erase heading not required.)

Place	Date	Hour	Summary of Events and Information	Remarks and references to Appendices
			II	
	3/5/17		'D' Coy. (2/Lt. J.W. CORBETT) was drawn up in two lines, 60 yards in rear. The formation was two waves, each of two lines, 10 yds between lines and 60 yards between waves – with 'D' Coy. as moppers up. The 9th Bn Linc Regt attacked on the left of the Battalion. On the right the flank was secured by the possession of the HINDENBURG LINE as far as the BLOCK – beyond this the flank was to be secured by the 64th Inf Bde. Bombing attack down the line.	
			The morning was very dark – sunrise was not until 5.23 a.m (summer time), the dust and smoke from our own barrage and that of the enemy which opened almost simultaneously making it impossible to see more than a few yards ahead.	
			Direction was lost rather early and the line swung over to the right – having compelled thereto by the 18th Division on the left, crossing the front of the 9th Bn and pressing them to the right. By 6.30 a.m it became evident that the attack had failed. No progress had been made by the 64th Inf Bde Bombers in the HINDENBURG LINE and the front of the 8th Bn was outflanked – in parts surrounded, and with a prospect of being cut off. The left flank (C Company) had been held up by excessive M.G. fire and took up a position in the sunken road running into FONTAINE-lez-CROISILLES through U1 b	

Instructions regarding War Diaries and Intelligence Summaries are contained in F. S. Regs., Part II. and the Staff Manual respectively. Title pages will be prepared in manuscript.

WAR DIARY
or
INTELLIGENCE SUMMARY.
(Erase heading not required.)

Army Form C. 2118.

Place	Date	Hour	Summary of Events and Information	Remarks and references to Appendices
			III	
	3/5/17		The remainder of the Battalion were on a line roughly 300 yards south of the jumping-off place - BROWN TRENCH T.6.a. N36 c & d to road in O.31.c. Here the Battalion remained and at about 11-30 a.m. it was reinforced by the 6th Bn. Leicestershire Regt. This line was held throughout the day and consolidated. No assistance was given by the two Tanks in the attack, both of them breaking down.	
			The following casualties were suffered by the Battalion during this action - Officers - CAPT A G ASTLE and 2nd LT. F E PRATLEY killed. MAJOR T L WARNER, 2nd LT G B JOHNSON, 2nd LT. R S HARRIS, 2nd LT R L SENNETT, and 2nd LT. P H HILL wounded. LT F R OLIVER - Missing believed wounded and Prisoner of War. 2nd LT F W H CLARKE - wounded and Prisoner of War. 2nd LTs. F B PITTS and W HARRIS - Prisoners of War. Other Ranks - Killed 19, Wounded 101, Missing 168, Died of Wounds 3. Total - 11 Officers, 291 Other Ranks.	
	4/5/17		The 110th Inf Bde. was relieved at 7 p.m. by the 62nd Inf. Bde. the Battalion going into bivouacks at St LEGER	
ST. LEGER.	8/5/17		LT COL. G C I HERVEY took over the command of the Battalion from MAJOR H L BEARDSLEY.	
	9/5/17		The Battalion took over the ST LEGER LINE from 6th Bn. Leic Regt. Bn H.Q at T.22.a.25.35 - A Coy in Strong Point at T.16.c.3.2, 'B' Coy in Sunken Road - T.22.a.20.65 to T.22.a.20.50. 'C' Coy in bank T.22.a.20.25 to T.22.a.00.20.	

2353 Wt. W2544/1454 700,000 5/15 D. D. & L. A.D.S.S. Forms/C. 2118.

Instructions regarding War Diaries and Intelligence Summaries are contained in F. S. Regs., Part II. and the Staff Manual respectively. Title pages will be prepared in manuscript.

WAR DIARY
or
INTELLIGENCE SUMMARY.
(Erase heading not required.)

Army Form C. 2118.

Place	Date	Hour	Summary of Events and Information	Remarks and references to Appendices
			IV	
	9/5/17.		'D' Company in Sunken Road T.22 a. & c.	
BERLES-AU-BOIS	11/5/17.		The ~~[illegible]~~ Division was relieved by the 33rd Division, the 1st Bn Queen's taking over the ST LEGER LINE from the Battalion. On relief the Battalion marched to rest billets at BERLES-AU-BOIS. From the 13th to the 23rd the Battalion fired a Course of Musketry, a competition being arranged by LT. COL G C I HERVEY, in which great interest was shown. From the 25th onwards, Field Training and Tactical Schemes were carried ~~at~~ out.	
	24/5/17.		The 110th Inf Bde Sports took place in the afternoon of this date, on an open piece of ground NORTH of the BIENVILLERS–MONCHY ROAD. Fine weather prevailed and an excellent programme was successfully carried through.	
	25/5/17.		The Battalion was inspected by the Divisional Commander, MAJOR GENERAL D G M CAMPBELL C.B.	
	28/5/17.		The Battalion was inspected by the VII Corps Commander LIEUT-GENERAL SIR T. D'O. SNOW. K.C.B.	

[illegible] Hervey Lt-Colonel
Comdg 8th Leicestershire Regt.

2353 Wt. W2544/1454 700,000 5/15 D. D. & L. A.D.S.S./Forms/C. 2118.

8th Bn Leicestershire Regiment

8th Leicester Regt

Instructions regarding War Diaries and Intelligence Summaries are contained in F. S. Regs., Part II. and the Staff Manual respectively. Title pages will be prepared in manuscript.

WAR DIARY
or
INTELLIGENCE SUMMARY.
(Erase heading not required.)

Army Form C. 2118.

References Sheet 51B S W 1/20000
LENS 11

Vol 21

Place	Date	Hour	Summary of Events and Information	Remarks and references to Appendices
HAMELINCOURT	1/6/17		The Battalion left BERLES-AU-BOIS where it had been in a period of rest for three weeks, and marched to HAMELINCOURT, where it bivouacked in tents in T 34 b. Training in Bombing, Rifle Grenades and Field Exercises was carried out until the 7th.	
HAMELINCOURT	7/6/17		MAJOR H.E.C. ANDERSON, 9th Bn Leic Regt, took over the command of the Battalion from LT. COL G.C.I. HERVEY who proceeded to ENGLAND.	
			On the night of the 7/8th the Battalion relieved the 13th Bn ~~Lancashire~~ Northumberland Fusiliers in the HINDENBURG LINE. The Battalion Sector extended from junction of PLUM LANE and HUMBER TRENCH, U 7 d 2.3. along HUMBER TRENCH, LUMP LANE to SENSEE RIVER inclusive, U 7 b. 15.70. Order of Companies in the line from right to left A.B.C.D. Battalion Headquarters in the Chalk Quarry at T.18 b 8.1.	
CROISILLES	11/6/17		On the night of the 11th the Battalion was relieved from the front line by the 6th Bn Leicestershire Regt and on relief proceeded into Brigade Reserve W of the village of CROISILLES. Battn Headquarters in Sunken Road T 22 d 8.9. A Company in Sunken Road, in T 22 c, B Company in No 5 POST T 22 a 2.8 C & D Companies in Trench T 23 c. Four quiet days were spent here, the Battalion furnishing working parties for the trench each night	

2353 Wt. W2544/1454 700,000 5/15 D. D. & L. A.D.S.S. Forms/C. 2118.

Instructions regarding War Diaries and Intelligence Summaries are contained in F. S. Regs., Part II. and the Staff Manual respectively. Title pages will be prepared in manuscript.

WAR DIARY
or
INTELLIGENCE SUMMARY.
(Erase heading not required.)

Army Form C. 2118.

Place	Date	Hour	Summary of Events and Information	Remarks and references to Appendices
	15/6/17		II On the night of the 15/16th the Battalion moved forward and took up positions in LINCOLN TRENCH, U 12 a & b, preparatory to the attack on TUNNEL TRENCH by the 12th & 13th Northd Fusiliers in the early morning of the 16th. Battalion Headquarters in the Quarry at T.18 b 8.1. Prior to the Battalion moving off the enemy put up a very heavy barrage on the village of CROISILLES on the ground between the village and the front line and on all approaches to the trenches. This barrage commenced at 9.30 pm and finished at 0.45 am 16/6/17. Owing to the heaviness of the barrage two companies of the 13th Northumberland Fusiliers were delayed in the march up to the front line and as a consequence when 'C' Company arrived in BURG TRENCH to take up the position of counter attacking Company they received instructions to go forward at once and go over the top with the three Companies 13th Northumberland Fusiliers who were already in position, one Company having been effectually delayed. Owing to the congestion of the very narrow trenches CAPT. MATTHEWS experienced great difficulty in getting 'C' Company into HUMBER TRENCH (front line)	

2353 Wt. W2544/1454 700,000 5/15 D. D. & L. A.D.S.S./Forms/C. 2118.

Instructions regarding War Diaries and Intelligence Summaries are contained in F. S. Regs., Part II. and the Staff Manual respectively. Title pages will be prepared in manuscript.

WAR DIARY
or
INTELLIGENCE SUMMARY.
(Erase heading not required.)

Army Form C. 2118.

Place	Date	Hour	Summary of Events and Information	Remarks and references to Appendices
			III	
			and finally led them from BURG TRENCH over the top to HUMBER TRENCH in time for the front platoon under LIEUT F HAINES to go forward with the remainder of the line. The second platoon under 2/Lt GREGORY was eventually able to go forward with the 2nd wave.	
			The whole attack was held up at the enemy wire by an intense machine gun barrage, the wire also had not been cut and it is estimated that there were double machine guns placed at intervals of only about twenty or thirty yards in TUNNEL TRENCH	
			At 5.30 a.m. the attacking force was compelled to withdraw this being twenty minutes after the Zero hour 5.10 a.m.	
			In connection with the engagement the following awards were made for gallantry – MILITARY MEDAL, Cpl J W BRIGGS and PTE G DYER both of 'C' Company	
	16/6/17		In the afternoon of the 16th the Battalion took over the front line from the 13th Bn Northumberland Fusiliers. A Company was on the right from junction of CURRANT LANE with HUMBER TRENCH U 7 d 35 10 to junction of PEAR LANE	

2353 Wt. W2544/1454 700,000 5/15 D. D. & L. A.D.S.S. Forms/C 2118.

Instructions regarding War Diaries and Intelligence Summaries are contained in F. S. Regs., Part II. and the Staff Manual respectively. Title pages will be prepared in manuscript.

WAR DIARY
or
INTELLIGENCE SUMMARY.
(Erase heading not required.)

Army Form C. 2118.

Place	Date	Hour	Summary of Events and Information	Remarks and references to Appendices
			IV	
			and HUMBER TRENCH, U 7 d 25 45 'C' Company in the centre from the point U 7 d 25 45 to junction of CHERRY LANE and HUMBER TRENCH U 7 d 2 6, and 'B' Company from U 7 d 2 6 to junction of HUMBER TRENCH and LUMP LANE, U 7 d 15 90. 'D' Company were in support in BURG TRENCH to the rear of HUMBER TRENCH. On the night of the 16th Battalion Headquarters were moved from the Quarry T 18 b 8 1 to a deep dugout in PLUM LANE U 7 d 15 30.	
	19/6/17		On the morning of the 19th 'D' Company relieved a Company of the 6th Battn Lincolnshire Regiment who were holding LUMP LANE.	
HAMELINCOURT	19/6/17		On the night of the 19th the Division was relieved by the 33rd Division, the Battalion being relieved by the 20th Battn Royal Fusiliers and on relief proceeded into camp at HAMELINCOURT. During its tour in the line the Battalion sustained the following casualties: Officers - CAPT. S POOL and 2/LT. MEDCALF killed, LIEUT F HAINES missing, 2/LT. H.H. DUVALL wounded - Other ranks - killed 7, wounded 23, missing 6	
BLAIRVILLE	21/6/17		On this day the Battalion moved into rest at BLAIRVILLE, where a programme of TRAINING was carried out	

2353 Wt. W3544/1454 700,000 5/15 D. D. & L. A.D.S.S./Forms/C. 2118.

Instructions regarding War Diaries and Intelligence Summaries are contained in F. S. Regs., Part II. and the Staff Manual respectively. Title pages will be prepared in manuscript.

WAR DIARY
or
INTELLIGENCE SUMMARY.
(Erase heading not required.)

Army Form C. 2118.

Place	Date	Hour	Summary of Events and Information	Remarks and references to Appendices
			V	
BLAIRVILLE	25/6/17		MAJOR A. T. LE M UTTERSON took over the command of the Battalion from MAJOR H. E. C. ANDERSON	

[illegible signature]
Lt. Col. Cmdg.
8th (S.) Battn Leicestershire Regiment

30 - 6 - 17

2353 Wt. W2544/1454 700,000 5/15 D. D. & L. A.D.S.S./Forms/C. 2118.

8th (Ser) Battn Leicestershire Regt — 21/110

Instructions regarding War Diaries and Intelligence Summaries are contained in F. S. Regs., Part II. and the Staff Manual respectively. Title pages will be prepared in manuscript.

WAR DIARY
or
INTELLIGENCE SUMMARY.
(Erase heading not required.)

Army Form C. 2118.

Reference Sheet 57c S.W. & Trench Map 1/20000 1/10000

Vol 22

Place	Date	Hour	Summary of Events and Information	Remarks and references to Appendices
	1/7/17		The Battalion left BLAIRVILLE (Reference LENS 11) and marched to CAMP A. S.E. of HAMELINCOURT S. 35. a. Platoon and Company Training was carried out during the seven days in which the Battalion was in camp. In the absence of Lieut. Col. A. T. le M. Utterson, D.S.O. the Battalion was under the command of Captain J. B. Matthews M.C. The 110th Infantry Brigade was in Divisional Reserve during this period.	
Vicinity of CROISILLES	8/7/17		In the afternoon of the 8th the ~~Brigade~~ 110th Infantry Brigade relieved the 64th Infantry Brigade holding the right sub. sector of the Divisional front, the 8th Battn Leicestershire Regt. moving into Brigade Support in the vicinity of CROISILLES. Dispositions of the Battalion as follows:– Battn Headquarters in Sunken Road, T 22 d. 9 9. A B and D Companies in trenches in T 23. a & c. C Company in Sunken Road T. 23 a. 20 65 – T 23 a. 5 9. Working and carrying parties in the forward area were supplied by the Battalion. Lieut. Col. A T le M. Utterson re-joined the Battalion on the 8th and took over the command of the Battalion.	
Front Line	14/7/17		The Battalion relieved the 6th Battn Leicestershire Regiment in the left sub-sector, right boundary CURRANT LANE, U 7 d 35 10 exclusive, left boundary SENSEE RIVER U 7 b 15 70.	

(A7092). Wt. W12839/M1293. 750,000. 1/17. D. D. & L., Ltd. Forms/C.2118/14.

Instructions regarding War Diaries and Intelligence Summaries are contained in F. S. Regs., Part II. and the Staff Manual respectively. Title pages will be prepared in manuscript.

WAR DIARY
or
INTELLIGENCE SUMMARY.
(Erase heading not required.)

Army Form C. 2118.

II

Place	Date	Hour	Summary of Events and Information	Remarks and references to Appendices
			HUMBER TRENCH Order of Companies in the line, from right to left – 'A' Company CURRANT LANE, U 7 d 35 10 – PEAR LANE U 7 d. 25 40 exclusive 'C' Company PEAR LANE U 7 d 25 40 inclusive – the junction of HUMBER TRENCH and LUMP LANE, U 7 d. 05 88. 'D' Company in LUMP LANE, 'B' Company in HIND TRENCH, U 7 d. 02 88 – SENSEE RIVER U 7 a 7 6. A forward post at U 7 b 15 70, was held by a Platoon of 'B' Company each night. On the night July 14/15 the enemy opened a short but heavy bombardment on the Battalion Sector, artillery and trench mortars being employed. A number of casualties were caused including 2nd Lieut J. W. Corbett 'A' Company who was killed while on duty in the front line. The remainder of the tour was comparatively quiet. On the night of the 15/16th 2nd Lieut W. A. Rowley, A Company was killed when in charge of a covering party. This officer through some mistake, made his way through the enemy wire and was shot in the inside of it by a hostile sentry.	
Vicinity of CROISILLES	20/7/17		The Battalion was relieved in the front line and on relief proceeded into Brigade Reserve, in the vicinity of CROISILLES. Disposition of the Battalion as follows – Battalion Headquarters in Sunken Road, T 22 d. 9 9.	

(A7092). Wt W12839/M1293. 750,000. 1/17. D. D. & L., Ltd. Forms/C.2118/14.

Instructions regarding War Diaries and Intelligence Summaries are contained in F. S. Regs., Part II. and the Staff Manual respectively. Title pages will be prepared in manuscript.

WAR DIARY
or
INTELLIGENCE SUMMARY.
(*Erase heading not required.*)

Army Form C. 2118.

Place	Date	Hour	III Summary of Events and Information	Remarks and references to Appendices
			'A' Company in Sunken Road T.17.c.70.65 – T.17.a.40.15. 'B' and 'D' Companies in Sunken Road T.22.c.5.5 – T.22.a.15.65. 'C' Company in shelters in Bank T.22.a.30.25 – T.23.a.0.2. Working and carrying parties in the forward area were again supplied by the Battalion during the period of six days.	
Front line	26/7/17		The Battalion relieved the 6th Battalion Leicestershire Regt in the left sub-sector. Battalion boundaries and order of Companies in the front line as in the previous tour (see pages I and II). Hostile activity considerably less than during the previous tour.	

[illegible signature]
Lieut Col.
Commanding
8th (Ser) Battn. Leicestershire Regiment

31-7-17

(A7092). Wt W12839/M1293 75,0.0. 1/17. D. D. & L., Ltd. Forms/C.2118/14.

8th Leicester Regt.

Instructions regarding War Diaries and Intelligence Summaries are contained in F. S. Regs., Part II. and the Staff Manual respectively. Title pages will be prepared in manuscript.

WAR DIARY
or
INTELLIGENCE SUMMARY.
(Erase heading not required.)

Army Form C. 2118.

Reference Sheet 51 B S.W - 5A and LENS 11

Vol 23

Place	Date	Hour	Summary of Events and Information	Remarks and references to Appendices
MOYENVILLE	1/8/17		The Battalion was relieved in the front line (TUNNEL SECTOR) during the afternoon, by the 15th Bn Durham Light Infantry, and on relief proceeded to Camp A, MOYENVILLE, S 35 a. The 110th Infantry Brigade was then in Divisional Reserve, and eight days were spent out of the line, during which time a programme of ~~work~~ training was carried out	
FORWARD AREA	9/8/17		On this day the 110th Infantry Brigade moved up into the front line the 8th Bn Leicestershire Regiment, being in Brigade Support the four Companies were disposed as follows.-	
			'A' Company in the QUARRY at T.18.b.8.3. 'B' Company in PLATOON POSTS Nos 6-10 in squares T.4, T.10, and T.16 'C' Company in HIND TRENCH from T.6.a.0.4 to T.6.d.8.1. 'D' Company in Sunken Road T.23.a.20.65 to T.23.a.5.9. Battalion Hqrs in Sunken Road at T.22.d.8.9. A, C and D Companies supplied working parties to the front line Battalion each night	
ERVILLERS	17/8/17		In the afternoon of the 17th the Battalion was relieved by the 1st Bn Lincolnshire Regiment, and on relief marched to a Hutment Camp at ERVILLERS. Platoon and Company Training was carried out during the time the Battalion was in rest	
BARLY S E of AVESNES-le-COMTE	25/8/17		The Battalion left ERVILLERS in the morning of the 25th and proceeded by Motor Lorries to BARLY Route ERVILLERS - BOYELLES - BEAURAINS - ARRAS -	

(A7092). Wt W12839/M1293 75,000. 1/17. D. D. & L., Ltd. Forms/C.2118/14.

Instructions regarding War Diaries and Intelligence Summaries are contained in F. S. Regs., Part II. and the Staff Manual respectively. Title pages will be prepared in manuscript.

WAR DIARY
or
INTELLIGENCE SUMMARY.
(*Erase heading not required.*)

Army Form C. 2118.

Place	Date	Hour	Summary of Events and Information	Remarks and references to Appendices
BARLY	25/8/17		DAINVILLE - BEAUMETZ - LEZ - LOGES II - MONCHIET - GOUY - EN - ARTOIS - FOSSEUX - BARLY. The night of the 25th was spent at this village, the Battalion being in billets.	
AMBRINES	26/8/17		The Battalion left BARLY and marched to AMBRINES via AVESNES - LE - COMTE and GIVENCHY - LE - NOBLE. A programme of Platoon, Company and Field Training was carried out until the 31st	
			31 - 8 - 17	
			[signature] Lt - Col Commanding 8th (Ser) Battn. Leicestershire Regt	

(A7092). Wt W12839/M1293. 750,000. 1/17. D. D. & L., Ltd. Forms/C.2118/14.

8th Battn Leicestershire Regt — 110

Instructions regarding War Diaries and Intelligence Summaries are contained in F. S. Regs., Part II. and the Staff Manual respectively. Title pages will be prepared in manuscript.

WAR DIARY
or
INTELLIGENCE SUMMARY.
(Erase heading not required.)

Reference
Lens 11
Hazebrouck 5A
Belgium & France Sheet 28

Army Form C. 2118.

8th Leicester R
Vol 24

Place	Date	Hour	Summary of Events and Information	Remarks and references to Appendices
AMBRINES	1/9/17		On 1st September the Battalion was in billets at AMBRINES N.W. of AVESNES-LE-COMTE (LENS 11) where a programme of training was carried out	
AVESNES-LE-COMTE	4/9/17		The Battalion ~~moved~~ marched to AVESNES-LE-COMTE on the afternoon of the 4th and was billeted in the town, where it remained until the 16th. During this period platoon company and battalion training was carried out according to programme	
CAESTRE	16/9/17		On the morning of the 16th the Battalion marched from AVESNES ~~to~~ via LE HAMEAU and TILLOY-les-HERMAVILLE to SAVY (LENS 11) W of AUBIGNY. Here the Battalion entrained, and after a four hours journey via LILLERS and HAZEBROUCK, arrived at CAESTRE, N.E of HAZEBROUCK (HAZEBROUCK 5A). The Battalion detrained and marched to a camp on the southern side of the village. A week was spent here, during which time training was continued	
METEREN	23/9/17		The Battalion marched to METEREN, two kilometres W of BAILLEUL, on the morning of the 23rd, and encamped outside the village on the northern side.	
ST HUBERTUSHOEK H 32.C 3 4.	26/9/17		The Battalion marched to FONTAINE HOUCK, N of METEREN (HAZEBROUCK 5A) and after embussing there proceeded via METEREN, BAILLEUL, LOCRE, and LA CLYTTE to HALLEBAST, H.32.d.8 2 (BELGIUM and FRANCE, SHEET 28). At this point the Battalion	

Instructions regarding War Diaries and Intelligence Summaries are contained in F. S. Regs., Part II. and the Staff Manual respectively. Title pages will be prepared in manuscript.

WAR DIARY
or
INTELLIGENCE SUMMARY.
(Erase heading not required.)

Army Form C. 2118.

Place	Date	Hour	Summary of Events and Information	Remarks and references to Appendices
			II	
			debussed, and marched into camp S of ST. HUBERTUSHOEK at H.32.c.3.4.	
RIDGE WOOD H.35c9.3.	29/9/17		On the morning of the 29th the Battalion marched to RIDGE WOOD, H.35c.9.3 (BELGIUM AND FRANCE, SHEET 28), and encamped at the N.W. edge of the wood. The Battalion remained in this camp until the night of September 30th/October 1st	
			[signature] Lt-Col Commanding 8th (Ser) Battn Leicestershire Regiment	
			30-9-17	

2353 Wt. W2544/1454 700,000 5/15 D. D. & L. A.D.S.S./Forms/C. 2118.

8th Bn Leicestershire Regt.

Instructions regarding War Diaries and Intelligence Summaries are contained in F. S. Regs., Part II. and the Staff Manual respectively. Title pages will be prepared in manuscript.

WAR DIARY or INTELLIGENCE SUMMARY.

(Erase heading not required.)

Army Form C. 2118.

11/21 Reference
BELGIUM Sheet 28 N.W.
ZILLEBEKE Sheets 28 NW 4 & NE 3 (part)
GHELUVELT 28 NE 3. HAZEBROUCK 5a

Vol 25

Place	Date	Hour	Summary of Events and Information	Remarks and references to Appendices
RIDGE WOOD H.35.c.9.3	30/9/17		On the afternoon of this date, the Battalion less Nucleus Party left RIDGE WOOD CAMP en route for the front line. Route. KRUISSTRAATHOEK, SHRAPNEL CORNER, TRANSPORT FARM, ZILLEBEKE LAKE, where a halt of two hours duration was made. At 6.30 p.m. the march was resumed via ZILLEBEKE, SANCTUARY WOOD, CLAPHAM JUNCTION, and BLACK WATCH CORNER. The Battalion relieved the 15th Bn Australian Infantry in the front line, dispositions as follows - 'C' Company on the left in shell holes and isolated portions of trenches, forming a rough line from J.10.b.50.32. to J.10.d.35.80. 'B' Company on the right from J.10.d.35.80 to J.10.d.35.50 also in shell holes. The Company Headquarters of these two front line Companies were in a line of concrete shelters at J.10.d.1.7. On the left flank of the Battalion were the Royal Welch Fusiliers (7th Division) and on the right flank, 9th Bn Leicestershire Regiment.	
			'D' Company was in support to the left front line Company, in shell holes approx. J.10.a.8.2. 'A' Company in support to the right front line Company in isolated trenches and shell holes approx J.10.c.45.50. Battalion Headquarters and 'A' Company Headquarters were in a line of concrete shelters along the road in J.10.c. central.	
			Relief was complete about 10 p.m. with no casualties.	
FRONT LINE	1/10/17		The night was extremely quiet, the absence of hostile shelling was particularly noticeable. At 5.30 a.m. a heavy hostile barrage was placed on the front line and 100 yards ~~E~~ W of the road in J.10.c. central. This was maintained until 6 a.m., when it became evident that a hostile counter attack on the 9th Battalion was in progress.	

(A7092). Wt. W12839/M1293. 750,000. 1/17. D. D. & L., Ltd. Forms/C.2118/14.

Army Form C. 2118.

Instructions regarding War Diaries and Intelligence Summaries are contained in F. S. Regs., Part II. and the Staff Manual respectively. Title pages will be prepared in manuscript.

~~WAR DIARY~~
or
INTELLIGENCE SUMMARY.

(Erase heading not required.)

Place	Date	Hour	Summary of Events and Information	Remarks and references to Appendices
			II	

The S.O.S. was sent up by the 9th Battalion on the right also by this Battalion, and a heavy barrage was placed on and in front of the enemy lines. Heavy Lewis Gun and Rifle fire was immediately brought to bear on the threatened flank. A few minutes after six a.m., a message was received from the 9th Battalion that the enemy had gained possession of their front line.

About 6-30 a.m. small parties of the enemy were seen ~~—~~ about JOIST FARM, J.10 d. 2.0. moving by short rushes towards our right front line Company and threatening to turn the right flank of the Battalion. Heavy Lewis Gun and Rifle fire was opened on the enemy who suffered casualties & were unable to make any progress down the slope towards the front line. About this time the intensity of our barrage lessened and towards 7 o'clock ceased altogether.

Between 7 a.m. and 10-30 a.m. the enemy made repeated attempts to advance against the open flank of the Battalion but was driven back on each occasion by Rifle and Lewis Gun fire. During this period, it was found that the 9th Bn Leic Regt had been reinforced by two companies of the 7th Bn Leic. Regt and were holding the line of the road running N and S in J.10.a. A defensive flank was formed from the right flank of D Company, J.10.d. 35.50 to Battalion H.Q.s at J.10.c 5.5. The right support Company (A) moved up to the road and linked up with Battalion Headquarters on the left and the left company of the 9th Battalion on the right.

At 10-45 a.m. ~~the battn~~ Captain J.B. MATTHEWS with the left support Company (B) moved from its position J.10.a 3.2, in order to make a counter attack

(A7092) Wt. W12839/M1293. 750,000. 1/17. D. D. & L., Ltd. Forms/C.2118/14.

Instructions regarding War Diaries and Intelligence Summaries are contained in F. S. Regs., Part II. and the Staff Manual respectively. Title pages will be prepared in manuscript.

WAR DIARY
or
INTELLIGENCE SUMMARY.
(Erase heading not required.)

Army Form C. 2118.

Place	Date	Hour	Summary of Events and Information	Remarks and references to Appendices
			III	
			against the enemy, holding the high ground in the vicinity of JOIST FARM. Unfortunately CAPT. J.B. MATTHEWS, M.C. was killed instantly by a sniper when making a personal reconnaissance, preparatory to the attack, and at 10.30 a.m, the hostile artillery put down a heavy barrage on the E. side of POLYGON WOOD consequently the counter. thrust did not materialise.	
			This heavy hostile barrage was kept up until 1 p.m, at which hour the shelling ceased, but no further hostile attack took place.	
			At 2 p.m, small parties of the enemy were seen moving about the S.W. edge of JETTY WARREN, but were dispersed by rifle fire. Shortly afterwards a hostile M.G. ~~was~~ opened traversing fire along the road in J.10.c central, and LT-COL. UTTERSON D.S.O. was hit in the arm by a bullet.	
			At 3.10 p.m, a determined effort was made by the enemy, 10 or 12 strong, to move down the slope from JOIST FARM towards Battalion Headquarters, but this attempt was stopped by rifle fire from the Battalion H.Q. Concrete Emplacement, the enemy retiring & leaving several dead behind them. No further attempt to advance was made by the enemy & the remainder of the afternoon passed quietly.	
			At 6-10 p.m, the S.O.S. Signal was put up by the Brigade on the right and an exceptionally heavy barrage was placed on the enemy lines by our artillery. No hostile attack developed, & at 8 p.m the barrage ceased.	
			At 8.5 p.m the enemy attempted a counter attack against the Royal Welsh Fusiliers on the left, the S.O.S. was again sent up & a second barrage of an hours duration was placed on the enemy lines. The counter attack was beaten back with loss to the enemy.	

(A7092) Wt. W12859/M1293 750,000 1/17 D. D. & L., Ltd. Forms/C.2118/14.

Instructions regarding War Diaries and Intelligence Summaries are contained in F. S. Regs., Part II. and the Staff Manual respectively. Title pages will be prepared in manuscript.

WAR DIARY
or
INTELLIGENCE SUMMARY.

(Erase heading not required.)

Army Form C. 2118.

Place	Date	Hour	Summary of Events and Information	Remarks and references to Appendices
			IV	
			The remainder of the night passed quietly, and at dawn a protective barrage was formed by our artillery lasting for 45 minutes.	
FRONT LINE	2/10/17		With the exception of desultory shelling of POLYGON WOOD during the morning, the day passed quietly, the situation remained unchanged and the enemy made no attempt to carry out any further attack. MAJOR H.E.C. ANDERSON came up during the morning to take over the command of the Battn and early in the afternoon LT. COL. UTTERSON D.S.O. went down to the dressing station, after having remained for 24 hours in command of the Battalion with a wound in his right arm.	
SCOTTISH WOOD ~~RIDGE WOOD~~ CAMP (N.35.d. central) (Sheet 28)	2/10/17		On the night of Oct 2nd/3rd the ~~Battalion~~ 110th Inf Bde. was relieved by the 64th Inf. Bde, the 8th Battn. being relieved by the 3/4th Bn Queens. On relief the Battalion marched to ~~RIDGE~~ SCOTTISH WOOD CAMP, via BLACK WATCH CORNER, CLAPHAM JUNCTION, SANCTUARY WOOD, ZILLEBEKE and SHRAPNEL CORNER.	
	3/10/17		The day was spent in reorganising the Battalion and resting the men. During the two days the Battalion had spent in the line, casualties to 11 officers and 175 O.R. Killed CAPT. J.B. MATTHEWS M.C. 2nd LTS V.E. ELLINGHAM, A.H. HEARN, A. SHAW and H. ROBINSON. Wounded - LT. COL. A.T. le M. UTTERSON. D.S.O. 2nd LTS. A.W. SMITH (since Died of Wounds) EASTWOOD and G. MORRIS. Wounded and remaining at duty 2nd LTS. A.J. FLETCHER and H. JASPER.	
			CAPTS. E. DERBYSHIRE and C.A. PAYNE were wounded on the morning of Sept. 30th whilst making a reconnaissance of the front line with LT. COL. UTTERSON D.S.O. and the Company Commanders.	
do.	4/10/17		On this day the 8th and 9th Bns. Leic. Regt. were amalgamated on account of the weak state of the two Battalions and came under the command of MAJOR R.R. YALLAND, 6th Bn. Leic Regt. MAJ. H.E.C. ANDERSON proceeding to ENGLAND on the Senior Officers Course at ALDERSHOT.	

(A7092). Wt. W12839/M1293. 750,000. 1/17. D. D. & L., Ltd. Forms/C.2118/14.

Instructions regarding War Diaries and Intelligence Summaries are contained in F. S. Regs., Part II. and the Staff Manual respectively. Title pages will be prepared in manuscript.

WAR DIARY
or
INTELLIGENCE SUMMARY.
(Erase heading not required.)

Army Form C. 2118.

Place	Date	Hour	Summary of Events and Information	Remarks and references to Appendices
			V	
RAILWAY DUGOUTS ZILLEBEKE I.21.d.	5/10/17		At 6 p.m. on the 5th, the 8/9th Bn. moved from SCOTTISH WOOD CAMP to RAILWAY DUGOUTS, on the N side of the railway embankment in I.21.d (Ref. ZILLEBEKE 1/10000). The 7th Bn. Leic. Regt. were in dugouts on W side of ZILLEBEKE LAKE and the 6 Bn. Leic Regt in support at CLAPHAM JUNCTION.	
	7/10/17		On the night of Oct 7/8th the 8/9th Bn moved from RAILWAY DUGOUTS to relieve the 7th Bn, who were in ~~close~~ support to the front line. On relief the 7th Bn moved into the front line. Two companies of the 8/9th Bn moved up into the front line and came under the command of LT. COL ALDWORTH, 7th Bn. Leic. Regt. The remaining two companies were in support in a strong point at JOIST FARM. Bn. H.Q. also in the strong point.	
	8/10/17		On the night of Oct 8/9 a further change in the dispositions was made, the two companies in the front line remaining there, the two companies from JOIST FARM moving to JETTY TRENCH in J.10.b. and Battn H.Q. to a line of concrete emplacements J.10.c. central. The 8/9th Battn. remained in this position until the night of the 11/12th. The weather during the whole of the time was extremely wet and the men suffered severely in the open trenches shell holes, which in many cases were full of water. During this tour in the line 1 officer 2nd Lt. ROBINSON was killed and 2/LTS MERCER and POCHIN were wounded, and 53 O.R. were killed and wounded.	
ANZAC CAMP H.30.c.5.3 (Sheet 28)	11/10/17		During the afternoon of the 11th the 8/9th Battn. moved out of its reserve position and proceeded to ANZAC CAMP via BLACK WATCH CORNER, CLAPHAM JUNCTION, BIRR X ROADS, WARRINGTON ROAD and SHRAPNEL CORNER.	
LE CROQUET (HAZEBROUCK 5A)	12/10/17		On the afternoon of the 12th the 8/9th Battalion was dissolved into separate units and marched to OUDERDOM STATION and entrained there for LE CROQUET (HAZEBROUCK 5a) W of HAZEBROUCK. The Battn. detrained at EBBLINGHEM STATION & marched to LE CROQUET, arriving there at 11-30 p.m. On this day the Battn. came under the command of MAJ. T.L. WARNER D.S.O. The 13th/14th Oct was spent in resting the men and cleaning up of all kit and equipment.	On 13/10/17 Lt Col [illegible] D.S.O. handed over the command of the Battalion to MAJOR T. L. W[illegible] D.S.O.
CAMP AT H.36.a.6.7.	15/10/17		The Battalion moved from LE CROQUET to CAMP at H.36.a.6.7 (Sheet 28) on the morning of Oct 15th, the journey being made in Motor Lorries via EBBLINGHEM, HAZEBROUCK, BAILLEUL, LOCRE and KEMMEL.	
do.	17/10/17 to 22/10/17		Cable Trench digging Parties were found daily by the Battalion for work in the forward areas between CLAPHAM JUNCTION and FITZCLARENCE FARM, J.14.d.45.95 (Ref. GHELUVELT). This work was carried out under very trying circumstances, the men working in heavy hostile barrages, and moving to and from the work under shell fire. The working parties were conveyed to and from the camp in Motor Lorries. Casualties - 1 officer wounded, 2/LT. F.E. FLOOD and 86 O.R. killed, wounded and missing.	

(A7092). Wt. W12839/M1293. 750,000. 1/17. D. D. & L., Ltd. Forms/C.2118/14.

Instructions regarding War Diaries and Intelligence Summaries are contained in F. S. Regs., Part II. and the Staff Manual respectively. Title pages will be prepared in manuscript.

WAR DIARY
or
INTELLIGENCE SUMMARY.
(Erase heading not required.)

Army Form C. 2118.

Place	Date	Hour	Summary of Events and Information	Remarks and references to Appendices
			VI	
CAMP A. H.30.a.4.5.	23/10/17 to 28/10/17		On the morning of the 23rd the Battalion moved from its Camp at H.36.a.6.7 to CAMP A, H.30.a.4.5. (Ref. Sheet 28). A certain amount of training and reorganisation was carried out here, but wet weather interfered with outdoor ~~training~~ training.	
SUPPORT to the FRONT LINE.	28/10/17		The Battalion moved into support on the night of Oct 28th. 2 Companies C & D and Battn H.Q. were at CLAPHAM JUNCTION. 'A' Company at JOIST FARM J.10.d.24. in support to the Right Front Line Battn and B Company at J.14.d.15.80 & POLYGON BUTTE in support to the left front line company.	
RAILWAY DUGOUTS ZILLEBEKE	29/10/17 to 31/10/17		The Battalion was relieved on the night of Oct 29th by the 6th Bn. Leic Regt and on relief proceeded into Bde. Reserve. RAILWAY DUGOUTS - S.W. of ZILLEBEKE LAKE in I.21.c.	

[signature] Lt. Col.
Cmdg 8th (S) Bn. Leicestershire Regt

31-10-17

(A7092) Wt. W12839/M1293. 750,000. 1/17. D. D. & L., Ltd. Forms/C.2118/14.

8th Bn. ~~Leicestershire~~ Leicestershire Regt (1) — 8th Leicester Regt

Instructions regarding War Diaries and Intelligence Summaries are contained in F. S. Regs., Part II. and the Staff Manual respectively. Title pages will be prepared in manuscript.

WAR DIARY
or
~~INTELLIGENCE SUMMARY.~~
(Erase heading not required.)

Ref. Maps: ZILLEBEKE
GHELUVELT.
BELGIUM & FRANCE, Sheet 28.
HAZEBROUCK. 5.a.
LENS. 11.

Army Form C. 2118.

110/31

WO 26

Place	Date	Hour	Summary of Events and Information	Remarks and references to Appendices
ZILLEBEKE	31st Oct / 1st Nov		On the night of Oct 31st/Nov 1st the Battalion moved up into Support to CLAPHAM JUNCTION - A & B Coys being sent forward to the POLYGON WOOD area. Whilst at CLAPHAM JUNCTION C & D Coys were called upon to furnish two working parties of 100 strong to dig a cable trench from HOOGE CRATER to HOOGE TEST POINT.	Owing to the maps of this area being handed in co-ordinates could not be used.
CLAPHAM JUNCTION	1st/2nd		On the night of the 1st/2nd the battalion moved back into Bde reserve at the RAILWAY dugouts at ZILLEBEKE LAKE & remained there for a period of two days.	
ZILLEBEKE LAKE	3rd/4th		On the night of the 3rd/4th the battalion relieved the 9th Bn Leicestershire Regt in the left sub-sector of the RIGHT Bde. Dispositions - A Coy on the R front. B Coy on the L front. B & C Coys in immediate support - Bn H.Q at POLYGONE BUTTE. Our front line extended from JUDGE COPSE to JUDGE COTT. inclusive. The immediate support was in the JOYCE FARM area. During this relief the Bn suffered heavy casualties owing to a hostile gas shell bombardment of CHATEAU WOOD, JARGON CROSS RDS & DEAD MULE CORNER. The battalion was in the line for 4 days - during this period the hostile activity was slight. Casualties for this tour - Officers - Capt C.A.B. ELLIOTT. 2/Lt R.L. SENNETT. & 2/Lt H. HEWSON O.R. 45. (Approaches to & from the line always heavily shelled with H.E & gas shells.)	
FRONT LINE	4th/5th		On the night of the 4th/5th the battalion was relieved by the 9th Bn Leicestershire Regt & moved back into Support at CLAPHAM JUNCTION - C & D Coys being left behind in the POLYGONE WOOD area	
CLAPHAM JUNCTION	Nov 5th		On the afternoon of the 5th the whole battalion moved back into Divisional reserve at Camp A. KRUISTRAATT. cross roads, & remained there for 4 days. During this period the battalion carried out the usual programme of training.	

(A7092). Wt. W12839/M1293. 750,000. 1/17. D. D. & L., Ltd. Forms/C.2118/14.

(2)

WAR DIARY
or
~~INTELLIGENCE SUMMARY~~.
(*Erase heading not required.*)

Army Form C. 2118.

Instructions regarding War Diaries and Intelligence Summaries are contained in F. S. Regs., Part II. and the Staff Manual respectively. Title pages will be prepared in manuscript.

Place	Date	Hour	Summary of Events and Information	Remarks and references to Appendices
CAMP. "A"	Nov 9th		On the afternoon of the 9th the battalion moved up into battalion support of the L Brigade at ZILLEBEKE BUND & remained there for 2 days.	
ZILLEBEKE BUND	11th/12th		On the night of the 11th/12th the battalion relieved the 9th Bn Leicestershire Regt in the R. Sub Sector of the L Brigade - Dispositions - C Coy on the right front - A Coy in the centre front - D Coy on the left front. B Coy in immediate support. Bn. H.Q was at POLYGONE BUTTE. The battalion was in the line for 2 days - during which period the hostile activity was slight - Casualties for this tour - 2/Lt A.K. WIFFEN - 2/Lt G.W. BEASLEY. O.R. 8.	
FRONT LINE	14th/15th		On the night of the 14th/15th the battalion was relieved by the 3rd Bn Wellington Regt - NEW ZEALAND division & moved back into support at ZILLEBEKE BUND.	
ZILLEBEKE BUND	Nov 16th		On the afternoon of the 16th the battalion marched to PIONEER CAMP - SCOTTISH WOOD area & remained there for the night.	
SCOTTISH WOOD area	Nov 17th		On the morning of the 17th the battalion marched to DEVONSHIRE CAMP, RENINGHELST - route via OUDERDOM & remained there for the night.	
RENINGHELST area	Nov 18th		On the morning of the 18th the battalion marched to LA BERCQUE - S.E of BAILLEUL - route via RENINGHELST - LA CLYTTE - LOCRE - BAILLEUL. On arriving the battalion went into billets.	
LA BERCQUE	Nov 19th		On the morning of the 19th the battalion marched to ARREWAGE - N of MERVILLE. Route via VER BERQUIN - LA CORONNE - CAUDESCRE. The battalion remained there the night in billets.	
ARREWAGE	Nov 20th		On the morning of the 20th the battalion marched to BELLERIVE - N.W. of BETHUNE - route via MERVILLE - CALONNE-sur-LIS - MONT BERNECHONE. The battalion rested there for the night.	
BELLERIVE	Nov 21st		On the morning of the 21st the battalion marched to COUPIGNE - S of HERSIN. Route via VENDIN-lès-BETHUNE - ANNEZIN - BETHUNE - FOUQUIÈRE-lès-BETHUNE, remaining there for 6 days.	G.G.
COUPIGNE	Nov 22nd		No programme of work was carried out, except cleaning up & reorganising	

(A7092). Wt. W12839/M1293. 750,000. 1/17. D. D. & L., Ltd. Forms/C.2118/14.

(3)

Army Form C. 2118.

Instructions regarding War Diaries and Intelligence Summaries are contained in F. S. Regs., Part II. and the Staff Manual respectively. Title pages will be prepared in manuscript.

WAR DIARY
or
INTELLIGENCE SUMMARY.
(Erase heading not required.)

Place	Date	Hour	Summary of Events and Information	Remarks and references to Appendices
COUPIGNE	Nov 25th		On the morning of the 25th the battalion marched to MONCHY BRETTON area. Route via FRESVILLE CAUCOURT – BÉTHONSART. The battalion was billetted as follows. Bn H.Q. & 2 Coys at VILLIERS – BRULIN – 2 Coys at BETHONSART.	
MONCHY BRETTON area	Nov 30th		On the afternoon of the 30th the battalion had sudden orders to entrain at SAVY at 8 P.M. as the Division had been called upon to reinforce the line in the neighbourhood of CAMBRAI, on account of a German attack on a large scale.	G.G.

Nov 30th 1917.

T. Haines Lt. Col.
Cmdg 8th Bn Leicestershire Regt

(A7092). Wt. W12839/M1293. 750,000. 1/17. D. D. & L., Ltd. Forms/C.2118/14.

(1)

8th Bn The Leicestershire Regt

Instructions regarding War Diaries and Intelligence Summaries are contained in F. S. Regs., Part II. and the Staff Manual respectively. Title pages will be prepared in manuscript.

Dec 1917

WAR DIARY
or
INTELLIGENCE SUMMARY.
(Erase heading not required.)

Ref. Maps.
FRANCE. Sheet 62C 1/40,000
FRANCE. Sheet 62C N.E. 1/20,000
FRANCE. Sheet 57C S.E 1/20,000.

Army Form C. 2118.

9R27

Place	Date	Hour	Summary of Events and Information	Remarks and references to Appendices
In the train	Dec 1st		On the morning of the 1st the Battalion detrained at TINCOURT & marched to billets in COURCELLES. Instructions were received that the Battalion was to be in readiness to move at a quarter of an hour's notice. The orders came & the Battalion move off from COURCELLES at 2pm en route for the line. Route taken - TINCOURT - LONGAVESNES - VILLERS FAUCON - SAINT EMILIE. A long halt was made at VILLERS FAUCON - where tea was served.	
			The Battalion relieved the 4th Bn South Lancashire Regt (PIONEER BN.) (55th DIVISION) in the Support line - being in Support to the ~~left battalion of the~~ right Brigade. Dispositions as follows. A Coy - in the Railway cutting (shelters) in X.25.c. - B Coy - in trenches running from F.1.b.3.9. to F.1.b.5.5. - C Coy in trenches running from X.25.c.9.3. to F.1.b.3.9. - D Coy in trenches running from X.25.c.7.5. to X.25.c.9.3. Bn H.Q was in the Railway Cutting at X.25.c.55.30.	
SUPPORT LINE	Dec 2nd		On the morning of the 2nd Bn H.Q was moved to the Railway Embankment at F.1.d.8.7. The Battalion boundary was side-slipped to the right on this day also. The new line ran from X.25c.9.3 to F.2.c.3.6. C Coy on the left - B Coy in the centre - D Coy on the right - & A Coy occupied shelters in the Railway Cutting in F.2.c. The Battalion remained in Support for three days - during which period the hostile activity was very slight.	
FRONT LINE	Dec 3rd		On the night of the 3rd the Battalion relieved the 9th Bn Leicestershire Regt in the front line	G.G.

2353 Wt W2544/1454 700,000 5/15 D. D. & L. A.D.S.S./Forms/C. 2118.

(2)

WAR DIARY
or
INTELLIGENCE SUMMARY.
(Erase heading not required.)

Army Form C. 2118.

Instructions regarding War Diaries and Intelligence Summaries are contained in F. S. Regs., Part II. and the Staff Manual respectively. Title pages will be prepared in manuscript.

Place	Date	Hour	Summary of Events and Information	Remarks and references to Appendices
FRONT LINE	Dec 3rd		in the right Sub sector of the right Brigade. Dispositions as follows - D Coy in the front line - occupying platoon posts at X.27.d.05.15. - X.27.d 20.05. - F.3.b.30.95. - X.27.c.6.3 - X.27.c.00.25. Coy H.Q. was at X.26.d.3.0. - C. Coy was in immediate Support - occupying posts at - F.2.b.5.5. - F.2.b.4.3 - F.2.b.4.1. - Coy H.Q was at F.2.b.4.1. - A Coy was the left Support Company in a continuous trench running from F.2.a.75.50 to F.2.c.9.9 - Coy H.Q was at F.2.a 75.50. - B Coy was the right Support Company in trenches running from F.2.c.9.9. to F.2.d.1.2. - Coy H.Q was at F.2.d.0.5. Bn H.Q was at the Same place as for Support - i.e Shelters in Railway Embankment at F.1.d.8.7. The Battalion remained in the front line for five days - during which period the hostile activity was very slight.	
BDE RESERVE	Dec 8th		On the night of the 8th the Battalion was relieved by the 9th Bn Leicestershire Regt & moved back into Brigade reserve - Dispositions as follows - A & B Coys in cellars in EPEHY - C & D Coys in huts in VILLERS FAUCON. Bn H.Q was at E.28.b.30.95. During this period A & B Coys worked 6 hrs per day on improving the EPEHY village defences.	
FRONT LINE	Dec 12th		On the night of the 12th the Battalion relieved the 9th Bn Leicestershire Regt in the right Sub sector of the right Brigade. The Brigade boundary having been altered in the interval dispositions were as follows - A Coy - occupying platoon posts at X.26.b.20.95 - X.26.b.20.75. - X.26.b.25.50	G.G.

2353 Wt. W2544/1454 700,000 5/15 D. D. & L. A.D.S.S./Forms/C. 2118.

Instructions regarding War Diaries and Intelligence Summaries are contained in F. S. Regs., Part II. and the Staff Manual respectively. Title pages will be prepared in manuscript.

(3)

WAR DIARY
or
INTELLIGENCE SUMMARY.

(*Erase heading not required.*)

Army Form C. 2118.

Place	Date	Hour	Summary of Events and Information	Remarks and references to Appendices
FRONT LINE.			& X.25.b.25.25. Coy H.Q. was in a shelter in 14 WILLOWS ROAD at X.26.a.6.2. – B Coy was the right support Company & occupied trenches running from X.26.c.95.30 to X.26.d.0.6. – Coy H.Q was at X.26.d.0.9. D Coy was the left Support Company & occupied trenches running from X.26.a.4.3. to X.26.a.30.45. – & from X.26.a.6.3. to X.26 central – Coy H.Q was in a deep dugout on 14 WILLOWS ROAD at X.26.a.5.3. – C Coy was the Reserve Company & occupied platoon posts. running from X.26.c.5.0. to X.26.a.10.65 Coy H.Q. was in the same dugout as D Coy H.Q. The Battalion remained in the front line for 4 days.	
SUPPORT LINE	Dec 16th		On the night of the 16th the Battalion was relieved by the 9th Bn Leicestershire Regt & moved back into Battalion Support. Dispositions as follows:– A Coy occupied shelters in the Railway Embankment at F.2.c – B Coy occupied shelters in the Railway cutting in X.25.c – C & D Coys occupied cellars in EPEHY. Bn H.Q. was at F.1.c.50.85. During the period in Support the Battalion worked six hours per day on digging trenches round EPEHY & improving the defence of the village.	
FRONT. LINE	Dec 20th		On the night of the 20th the Battalion again relieved the 9th Bn Leicestershire Regt in the right Sub sector of the right Brigade. The position of the trenches were the same as the last tour & disposition of Coys were as follows:– C Coy in the front line posts – D Coy was the right Support Company – B Coy was the left Support Company – A Coy was the reserve Company	G.G.

(14)

Instructions regarding War Diaries and Intelligence Summaries are contained in F. S. Regs., Part II. and the Staff Manual respectively. Title pages will be prepared in manuscript.

WAR DIARY
or
INTELLIGENCE SUMMARY.
(Erase heading not required.)

Army Form C. 2118.

Place	Date	Hour	Summary of Events and Information	Remarks and references to Appendices
FRONT LINE	Dec 20th		On the night of the 20th one of our patrols (consisting of 1 N.C.O. & 3 men) failed to return. Two of the men of this patrol returned on the morning of the 24th & reported that they had encountered an enemy Patrol & that they feared that the N.C.O & the other man had been captured by the enemy. The Battalion was relieved by the 9th Bn Leicestershire Regt on the night of	
SAULCOURT	Dec 24th		the 24th & moved back into Brigade reserve at SAULCOURT into huts. The Battalion remained there for four days & most of the time was spent in cleaning up.	
FRONT LINE	Dec 28th		On the night of the 28th the Battalion relieved the 9th Bn Leicestershire Regt in the right sub sector of the right Brigade - Disposition of Companies as follows:- A Coy in the front line posts - B Coy was the right Support Company - D Coy was the left Support Company - C Coy was the reserve Company. Coy H.Q's & Bn H.Q. were as before. During this tour of duty the Battalion was informed of the death of Major T. L. Warner D.S.O on the 27th at the 55th C.C.S following an operation for appendicitis. He was taken ill when the Battalion was last in Support. The Battalion remained in the front line for 4 days.	G.G.
			T.C. Howitt Lt. Col. Cmdg. 8th Bn Leicestershire Regt	

2353 Wt. W2544/1454 700,000 5/15 D. D. & L. A.D.S.S./Forms/C. 2118.

APPENDIX

to

War Diary for the month of December 1917.

of

8th Bn. The Leicestershire Regiment.

I. During the whole of the time in the line the Battalion, together with the 9th Bn. Leicestershire Regt, dug & consolidated a new front line, immediate support line & support line. This was carried out under very trying weather conditions. A hard frost set in, which made digging, at times, almost impossible.

II. The enemy was kept under close observation throughout the period by means of patrols sent out – mostly in the hours of darkness – but sometimes in daylight.

III. The two men, who returned from the missing patrol, on the 24th (described on page 4 of the War Diary) brought back valuable information, concerning the work in progress by the enemy, opposite the Battalion sector.

IV. The enemy did not send out many patrols – in fact during the whole of the period the hostile activity was exceedingly slight.

V. The defences of EPEHY were considerably strengthened & improved. The Battalion also helped to put out a great deal of wire entanglements

T.C. Howitt Lt. Col.

Cmdg. 8th Bn. Leicestershire Regt.

8th (S) Bn. LEICESTERSHIRE REGT.

Page 1.

Instructions regarding War Diaries and Intelligence Summaries are contained in F. S. Regs., Part II. and the Staff Manual respectively. Title pages will be prepared in manuscript.

January 1918.

WAR DIARY
or
~~INTELLIGENCE SUMMARY.~~
(Erase heading not required.)

Army Form C. 2118.

Ref: FRANCE, sheet 57c S.E 1:20,000
FRANCE, sheet 62c N.E 1:20,000
FRANCE, sheet 62c – 1:40,000

Vol 28

Place	Date	Hour	Summary of Events and Information	Remarks and references to Appendices
SUPPORT (EPEHY)	Jan 1st 1918.		On the night of the 1st/2nd the Battalion was relieved by the 9th Bn Leicestershire Regiment in the front line & moved back into Bn Support in EPEHY. Dispositions were as follows:– A Coy & B Coy were accomodated in cellars in the village – C Coy was in the Railway cutting (shelters) in X.25.c – D Coy was in the Railway embankment (shelters) in F.2.c. Bn HQ. was situated in HIGH STREET, EPEHY. F1.a.30.15.	
MIDDLESEX CAMP, HEUDECOURT.	Jan 4th		On the night of the 4th/5th the 110th Inf Bde was relieved by the 64th Inf Bde. The Battalion was relieved by the 10th Bn K.O.Y.L.I. Regt on this night & moved back to MIDDLESEX CAMP, HEUDECOURT (Bde reserve). The Battalion was accomodated in huts etc. Lt Col. A.T. Le M. UTTERSON, D.S.O. again took over command of the Battn from this date. During the period the Battalion remained in HEUDECOURT, most of the time was spent in cleaning up & inspections etc.	
HAUT ALLAINES	Jan 11th		On the morning of the 11th the Battalion marched to HAUT ALLAINES & took over a camp there (approx: I.5.a.5.5.) – Route taken. FINS – NURLU – AIZECOURT LE HAUT – HAUT ALLAINES. Whilst there a programme of training was carried out, consisting of drill, tactical exercises, bombing, Lewis gun instruction, rifle range practice etc.	
SAULCOURT	Jan 16th		On the morning of the 16th the Battalion marched to a Camp in SAULCOURT at approximately E.9.d & E.15.b. The Battalion was accomodated in huts. One Coy from the 9th Bn Leicestershire Regt was attached to the Battalion whilst in SAULCOURT. Working parties were found for wiring, tunneling etc daily. Nine Lewis guns & teams were mounted on different transport lines for A.A. defence each night.	G.G.

(A7092) Wt W12839/M1293 750,000 1/17. D. D. & L., Ltd. Forms/C.2118/14.

Page 2.

8th (S.) Bn LEICESTERSHIRE REGT.

Instructions regarding War Diaries and Intelligence Summaries are contained in F. S. Regs., Part II. and the Staff Manual respectively. Title pages will be prepared in manuscript.

WAR DIARY
or
~~INTELLIGENCE SUMMARY.~~
(Erase heading not required.)

Army Form C. 2118.

Place	Date	Hour	Summary of Events and Information	Remarks and references to Appendices
FRONT LINE	Jan 20th		On the night of the 20th/21st the 110th Inf Bde relieved the 64th Inf Bde in the right Sector. This Battalion relieved the 1st Bn East Yorkshire Regt in the right Sub Sector. Dispositions were as follows:— "C" Coy in the front line – D Coy in the right Support B Coy in the left Support + A Coy in the reserve line – Exact positions were the same as described in the diary for the month of December – with the exception of 1 platoon of C Coy & 1 platoon of A Coy being respectively in cellars in EPEHY & shelters in the Railway embankment in F.1.d owing to the thaw making the trenches untenable. This was rectified after the Battn had been in the line two days.	
SAULCOURT (RESERVE)	Jan 24th		On the night of the 24th/25th the Battalion was relieved by the 9th Bn Leicestershire Regt & moved back into reserve at SAULCOURT. During the period in reserve a working party was found by the Battalion of 60 strong working under R.E Supervision daily.	
FRONT LINE	Jan 28th		On the night of the 28th/29th the Battalion again took over the right sub-sector of the right Bde from the 9th Bn Leicestershire Regt & remained in the front line for four days. During the whole of the month the hostile activity was very slight & the Battalion suffered no casualties. The weather was bad especially during the end of the month & the trenches were continually falling in	

[signature]
Lt Col. Cmdg
8th Bn Leicestershire Regt

G.G.

(A7092). Wt. W12839/M1293 75,000. 1/17. D. D. & L., Ltd. Forms/C.2118/14.

①

8th Bn Leicestershire Regt

Instructions regarding War Diaries and Intelligence Summaries are contained in F. S. Regs., Part II. and the Staff Manual respectively. Title pages will be prepared in manuscript.

WAR DIARY
or
INTELLIGENCE SUMMARY.
(Erase heading not required.)

Army Form C. 2118.

Feb 1918

Ref Map
FRANCE Sheet 62c 1:40,000
FRANCE Sheet 62c N.E. 1:20000
FRANCE Sheet 57c S.E. 1:20,000
FRANCE Sheet 57c 1:40000

Vol 29

Place	Date	Hour	Summary of Events and Information	Remarks and references to Appendices
FRONT LINE	Feb 1st/2nd	night	On the night of the 1st/2nd of Feb the Battalion was relieved in the front line by the 9th Bn Leicestershire Regt & moved back into Support in EPEHY. Dispositions - as for the Support in last months war diary. During this period the Battalion found working parties of 240 men per day for work under R.E. supervision.	
SUPPORT (EPEHY)	Feb 5th	afternoon	On the afternoon of the 5th the Battalion again took over the front line from the 9th Bn Leicestershire Regt in the right Sub-sector. Dispositions as follows - D Coy in the front line - C. Coy in right Support - A. Coy in left Support - B Coy in reserve. A great deal of work was done improving the trenches etc & each night a party of 50 men was found for work under the R.E's.	
FRONT LINE	Feb 9th	afternoon	On the afternoon of the 9th the 110th Infantry Brigade was relieved by the 64th Infantry Brigade in the Right Brigade Sector. The Battalion was relieved on this date by the 1st Bn East Yorkshire Regt & moved back by Centimetre Train to MOISLAINS for reorganisation & training. The Battalion was accomodated in Adrian Huts etc in YORK CAMP. A set programme of training was carried out whilst the Battalion was in MOISLAINS. On the morning of the 11th the 9th Bn Leicestershire Regt was disbanded & split up between the remaining three Battalions in the Brigade. One hundred & eighty three other rank & fifteen officers were posted to this	

A5092 Wt. W1285/M1293. 750,000. 1/17. D. D & L., Ltd. Forms/C2118/14.

(2)

Instructions regarding War Diaries and Intelligence Summaries are contained in F. S. Regs., Part II. and the Staff Manual respectively. Title pages will be prepared in manuscript.

WAR DIARY
or
INTELLIGENCE SUMMARY.
(Erase heading not required.)

Army Form C. 2118.

Place	Date	Hour	Summary of Events and Information	Remarks and references to Appendices
			Battalion	
YORK CAMP MOISLAINS	Feb 15th	Afternoon	On the afternoon of the 15th the Brigade was inspected by the Commander in Chief Field Marshal Sir Douglas Haig. He expressed his extreme satisfaction at the general condition & "turn out" of the men of this Brigade.	
			The Battalion remained in MOISLAINS for ten days.	
YORK CAMP MOISLAINS	Feb 19th	Morning	On the morning of the 19th the Battn moved to GURLU WOOD (A. Camp) near NURLU (V.28.d) for work on the GREEN LINE. Work commenced on the morning of the 19th. It consisted of digging a continuous fire trench to a depth of three foot. This was carried daily under the supervision of the 146th A.T. Coy. R.E. this Battalion supplying 300 men & working 6 hours daily. The Battalion had also a party of 2 officers + 50 other ranks detached at CARTIGNY for work on a new aerodrome. A party of 4 officers + 150 other ranks was also found every alternate day for work on new aerodrome near NURLU. This work consisted of filling in shell holes.	
A CAMP GURLU WOOD	Feb 24th	Morning	The Battalion moved from GURLU WOOD on the morning of the 24th for work on the Battle Zone under the supervision of the Pioneer Battalion of the 39th Division. Two Companies (A & B Coys) were accommodated in DESSART WOOD (near FINS) – Two Companies + Bn HQ were accommodated in DEVON CAMP HEUDECOURT.	
			The Battalion found approximately 550 men daily working 5 hrs. The work	

A7092. Wt. W128.9/M1293. 750,000. 1/17. D. D. & L., Ltd. Forms/C2118/14.

(3)

Army Form C. 2118.

Instructions regarding War Diaries and Intelligence Summaries are contained in F. S. Regs., Part II. and the Staff Manual respectively. Title pages will be prepared in manuscript.

WAR DIARY
or
INTELLIGENCE SUMMARY.

(Erase heading not required.)

Place	Date	Hour	Summary of Events and Information	Remarks and references to Appendices
			Consisted of improving the posts in front of the main line of defence (YELLOW LINE), deepening communication trenches & digging the main line of defence (YELLOW LINE) to the required depth. This work was done in the vicinity of PEIZIERE. On the afternoon of the 25th B Coy moved from DESSART WOOD to HEUDECOURT owing to hostile shelling.	
DEVON CAMP HEUDECOURT	Feb 28th	Afternoon	On the afternoon of the 28th the 110th Infantry Brigade relieve the 46th Infantry Brigade (16th Division) in the left Brigade Sector. The Battalion relieved the 7th Bn (South Irish Horse) I. H. in the right Sub Sector on this date	

A. Utterson Lt. Col
Cmdg 8th Bn Leicestershire Regt

A7092 Wt W12839/M1293 750,000 1/17 D. D & L. Ltd. Forms/C2118/14.

110th Inf.Bde.
21st Div.

WAR
DIARY

8th BATTN. THE LEICESTERSHIRE REGIMENT.

M A R C H

1 9 1 8

8th

8th Battn Leicestershire Regt

Reference — 110/21

Army Form C. 2118.

Instructions regarding War Diaries and Intelligence Summaries are contained in F. S. Regs., Part II. and the Staff Manual respectively. Title pages will be prepared in manuscript.

WAR DIARY
or
INTELLIGENCE SUMMARY.
(Erase heading not required.)

VALENCIENNES } 1:100000 { B 6
ST QUENTIN } { B 1
AMIENS
LENS 11

30

Place	Date	Hour	Summary of Events and Information	Remarks and references to Appendices
FRONT LINE E of EPEHY B 6	1-3-18		The 8th Battn relieved the 6th Battn Leic Regt in the front line on the night of March 1st. Relief was carried through without any disturbing incidents. The four companies were distributed in depth with one Company in reserve. Four quiet days were spent in the line; the usual work on trenches and defences was carried on and the attitude of the enemy gave no cause for any suspicion.	
EPEHY B 6	4-3-18		On the night of the 4th the Battalion was relieved by the 6th Battn Leic Regt and on relief became Brigade Support. Two companies to man the village defences were billeted in the village whilst companies for the defence of the main line of resistance viz. RED LINE east of EPEHY were accommodated in dugouts and shelters along the line of the railway E of the village. Battalion H.Q were in FISHER'S KEEP EPEHY. Four uneventful days were spent in	Support
FRONT LINE E of EPEHY B 6	8-3-18		The 8th Battn moved into the Front Line on the night of March 8th relieving the 6th Battn Leic Regt. The usual work on trenches and defences was carried on during the period of four days. During this tour in the line a change in the attitude of the enemy became apparent. Strong patrols were encountered or seen in No Mans Land, the hostile artillery made no reply to our shelling of his front line system or back areas and prisoners captured all spoke of an attack being in preparation. Prisoners statements were on the whole very contradictory, the stories and reports of an impending attack being frequently confirmed and denied. There was also no agreement as to the locality in which the hostile attack was to be delivered. Towards March 12th however it became practically certain from information received from all sources that a hostile attack was in course of preparation and approached the VII Corps front, the probable date being given as 14th 15th or 16th of March. On the afternoon of the 12th 2/Lt E A DOWES was killed in the front line by a sniper	

A.7092 Wt. W12839/M1293 750,000 1/17. D. D & L., Ltd. Forms/C2118/14.

Army Form C. 2118.

Instructions regarding War Diaries and Intelligence Summaries are contained in F. S. Regs., Part II. and the Staff Manual respectively. Title pages will be prepared in manuscript.

II

WAR DIARY
or
INTELLIGENCE SUMMARY.

(Erase heading not required.)

Place	Date	Hour	Summary of Events and Information	Remarks and references to Appendices
EPEHY B. 6	12-3-18		The Battalion was relieved in the front line on the night of the 12th by the 6th Battn. Leic. Regt and on relief became Brigade Support in EPEHY. Dispositions. two companies billeted in EPEHY for the defence of the village 1 company along the line of the railway E of the village for the defence of the RED LINE and 1 Company at SAULCOURT (ST QUENTIN · B.1) for counter attack purposes. Battalion H.Q in FISHERS KEEP EPEHY. The attitude of the enemy still remained very suspicious his artillery made no reply to our continued heavy bombardments of his front line system and back areas. and it was evident that the enemy desired to conceal the positions of his guns. Prisoners still continued to give information of an impending attack. Accordingly a scheme of special vigilance was prepared along the VII Corps front, which came into action on the receipt of the order 'Man Battle Stations' No attack developed on the morning of the 13th and in the afternoon of this day a change was made in the dispositions of the Support Battalion. Another Company was sent to SAULCOURT. two companies were left in EPEHY for the defence of that village and Battalion H.Q moved to SAULCOURT. The second Company at SAULCOURT was to be utilised for the defence of the YELLOW LINE, some 1000 yards W of EPEHY, moving up to this line on the order 'Man Battle Stations'. The counter attack Company also moved forward to the YELLOW LINE on receipt of this order and Battn. H.Q moved to a mined dugout on the EPEHY · VILLERS FAUCON ROAD. As a hostile attack was expected the whole Brigade stood to in the Battle Stations from 5 a.m. - 7 a.m. on the mornings of the 15th 16th and 17th of March. About 6 a.m. on the morning of the 17th the S.O.S. signal was seen on our right & heavy artillery fire was heard. The signal was repeated along the Divisional front & the 21st Divl artillery came into action	

A;092 Wt. W1289/M1293 750,000. 1/17. D. D & L., Ltd. Forms/C2118/14.

Instructions regarding War Diaries and Intelligence Summaries are contained in F. S. Regs., Part II. and the Staff Manual respectively. Title pages will be prepared in manuscript.

III

WAR DIARY
or
INTELLIGENCE SUMMARY.
(Erase heading not required.)

Army Form C. 2118.

Place	Date	Hour	Summary of Events and Information	Remarks and references to Appendices
			No enemy action took place on the Brigade or Divisional front and the artillery ceased fire about 6.20 a.m. Heavy artillery fire was heard some distance to the south up to 6.40 a.m. when the fire diminished and finally ceased. No hostile attack had developed and it is probable that the alarm was caused by the heavy hostile artillery fire to the south.	
FRONT LINE E of EPEHY B 6	17-3-18		The Battalion moved into the front line on the night of March 17th relieving the 6th Battalion Leic. Regt. The enemy's attitude still remained abnormal, and prisoners obtained by means of raids gave the date for the attack as the 20th 21st or 22nd. Hostile patrols were seen or encountered in No Man's Land and the extraordinary inactivity of the hostile artillery was still maintained. The weather was extremely fine, and had been so for the previous week. Under the warm and continued sunshine, the ground became very dry and firm. Heavy ground mists were prevalent during the early mornings. At 1 a.m. on the morning of the 21st, a patrol of 1 Officer and 20 Other Ranks was sent out by 'C' Company to obtain an identification. This patrol met with no opposition whatsoever and on his return the Officer in charge was able to report that not a single German had been seen. At 4.30 a.m. the hostile artillery ended its long period of inactivity and commenced a heavy bombardment of the Divisional front and to the north and south. H.E. and large quantities of gas shell were used on the frontline system, the village of EPEHY & the batteries. Very heavy shelling of villages in our back areas also took place, and it quickly became evident that the artillery preparation for an attack on a large scale was in progress.	

IV

Army Form C. 2118.

WAR DIARY
or
INTELLIGENCE SUMMARY.
(Erase heading not required.)

Instructions regarding War Diaries and Intelligence Summaries are contained in F. S. Regs., Part II. and the Staff Manual respectively. Title pages will be prepared in manuscript.

Place	Date	Hour	Summary of Events and Information	Remarks and references to Appendices
			The gas bombardment was particularly severe mustard gas being used, all ranks were compelled to wear their box respirators for at least 3 hours.	
			When daylight came just after 6 a.m. it was quite impossible to see the wire in front of the trenches on account of the thickness of the mist. A great disadvantage was thus experienced, the necessity for good observation being absolutely vital to the defenders.	
			Towards 9 a.m. the hostile artillery lifted the greater part of its fire from our frontline system, and placed a standing barrage W of EPEHY on the battery positions and all approaches. Telephone communication with two of the front line companies C & D was still working, and no enemy infantry attacks had been reported. The thick mist still continued and observation was impossible. During the preparatory bombardment very few casualties were sustained by the Battalion and all ranks were fully prepared for the appearance of the hostile infantry.	
			At 9.50 a.m. the enemy infantry advanced to the attack, in accordance with the order 'Man Battle Stations', the front line garrison had been withdrawn to the immediate Support Line, and the attack on the Battalion sector was everywhere repulsed with heavy loss to the enemy. The enemy was content to hold for the time our vacant front line, where he was subjected to a heavy and accurate rifle grenade and Lewis Gun fire. Visibility still continued to be impossible & F.O.O's were unable to inform their batteries of the position of the hostile infantry or even to give any clear idea of the situation.	

V

WAR DIARY
or
INTELLIGENCE SUMMARY.
(Erase heading not required.)

Army Form C. 2118.

Instructions regarding War Diaries and Intelligence Summaries are contained in F. S. Regs., Part II. and the Staff Manual respectively. Title pages will be prepared in manuscript.

Place	Date	Hour	Summary of Events and Information	Remarks and references to Appendices
			During the course of the morning the mist lifted slightly and at intervals strong forces of the enemy could be seen advancing towards RONNSOY and LEMPIRE on our right. The 16 Division on our right were compelled to withdraw some distance to conform with the line on their right. Strong bombing attacks were made against our right flank held by A Company, on two occasions the enemy forced their way into A Company's trenches but were immediately ejected by vigorous counter bombing.	
			Towards 1 p.m. a lull occurred in the fighting on the Battalion front and meanwhile the mist has cleared. Large forces of the enemy could be seen moving W through RONNSOY and LEMPIRE, and large concentrations of his infantry were seen massing in the valleys E of our front line and in the neighbourhood of VAUCELETTE FARM and VILLERS GUISLAIN.	
			During the afternoon reports received showed that the enemy has broken through our defensive system on the right and were advancing rapidly. The enemy was everywhere held on the 110th Brigade front.	
			Towards 5 p.m. the enemy commenced to trench mortar the support line, the fire being heavy and accurate, and at 6 p.m. a withdrawal was made to the RED LINE just E of EPEHY to conform with the 7th Bn Leic Regt on our left, who had been driven out of their support line, to link up with the left Battalion of the 16th Division on our right.	

VI

WAR DIARY
or
INTELLIGENCE SUMMARY.
(*Erase heading not required.*)

Army Form C. 2118.

Instructions regarding War Diaries and Intelligence Summaries are contained in F. S. Regs., Part II. and the Staff Manual respectively. Title pages will be prepared in manuscript.

Place	Date	Hour	Summary of Events and Information	Remarks and references to Appendices
			The night of March 21/22 passed without any further attack on the part of the hostile infantry, but the enemy artillery displayed great activity during the night chiefly on the approaches to EPEHY and the back areas.	
EPEHY – ALECOURT-LE-HAUT ~~[illegible]~~ GREEN LINE	22·3·18		The early morning of the 22nd brought with it the same heavy mist, the hostile artillery displayed little activity and up till 9 am the enemy made no further attack. Observation of any kind was quite impossible and the movements of the enemy on our right could not be seen. During the night of the 21/22 from information received it was evident that small parties of the enemy had reached the EPEHY - ST EMILIE ROAD, it was also reported that a small party about 20 strong had been seen near the abandoned Dressing Station on the S.W edge of EPEHY. About 9 a.m. favoured and hidden by the heavy mist the enemy infantry commenced to push into the village from the EPEHY - ST EMILIE ROAD. Three posts on the S.E. edge of the village were rushed from the rear and taken, and the enemy continued to advance in a N.E. direction through the village. By this time the right flank of the Battalion was completely in the air, & the hostile infantry were threatening the RED LINE from the E. S and W. The Commanding Officer decided to evacuate the RED LINE at 10 a.m., at the same time moving Battn H.Q. from FISHERS KEEP. Accordingly this decision was communicated to the 2 companies holding the RED LINE and to the 2 companies of the 6th Battn Leic Regt defending the village.	

A.7092. Wt W12839/M1293 750,000. 1/17. D. D & L., Ltd. Forms/C2118/14.

VII

WAR DIARY
or
INTELLIGENCE SUMMARY.
(Erase heading not required.)

Instructions regarding War Diaries and Intelligence Summaries are contained in F. S. Regs., Part II. and the Staff Manual respectively. Title pages will be prepared in manuscript.

Army Form C. 2118.

Place	Date	Hour	Summary of Events and Information	Remarks and references to Appendices
			The evacuation of the RED LINE was carried out under very difficult circumstances, as the enemy were rapidly closing in from three sides. A defensive flank was then formed along the SAULCOURT-EPEHY ROAD to link up with the 7th Battn Leic Regt holding PEIZIERE and the ~~YELLOW~~ LINE held by 2 Companies, 6th Bn Leic Regt and 2 companies of the Reserve Brigade.	
			About 10.30 a.m. the mist lifted considerably, very large forces of hostile infantry were seen advancing W along the high ground between VILLERS-FAUCON and EPEHY. It was very evident that the enemy would make a serious attempt to drive in the right flank of the YELLOW LINE.	
			Towards 11 a.m. small parties of the enemy infantry began to break clear of the W side of EPEHY and to collect together in the dead ground W of the village. These parties were made to pay dearly for their enterprise, but shortly after 11 a.m. the mist descended again & the enemy was able to complete his concentration in comparative safety.	
			At 11.30 a.m. the ~~7th Bn Leic Regt [illegible]~~ Brigade received orders to withdraw through SAULCOURT to LONGAVESNES (ST. QUENTIN A.1) and to reorganise there. At the same time the enemy, about a Battalion strong, pushed forward from EPEHY towards the SAULCOURT-EPEHY ROAD.	
			The Brigade slowly withdrew through the defences of SAULCOURT (BROWN LINE) held by the Reserve Brigade and details of 110th Bde. H.Q. to LONGAVESNES. From there the Brigade marched to AIZECOURT-LE-HAUT arriving there about 7 p.m.	
			In the meantime the enemy's advance was arrested by the SAULCOURT DEFENCES and the BROWN LINE W of SAULCOURT.	

A7092 Wt. W12839/M1293. 750,000. 1/17. D. D & L., Ltd. Forms/C2118/14.

VIII

Army Form C. 2118.

Instructions regarding War Diaries and Intelligence Summaries are contained in F. S. Regs., Part II. and the Staff Manual respectively. Title pages will be prepared in manuscript.

WAR DIARY
or
INTELLIGENCE SUMMARY.

(Erase heading not required.)

Place	Date	Hour	Summary of Events and Information	Remarks and references to Appendices
			At 4.30 p.m. after a short but very intensive artillery preparation the enemy made an attack in force on the BROWN LINE and succeeded in capturing SAULCOURT. After this rapid progress was made by the enemy, resulting in the loss of GUYENCOURT, LONGAVESNES and LIERAMONT. During the evening the Corps received orders to withdraw to the GREEN LINE E. of TEMPLEUX LA FOSSE, to conform with the movements of the next Corps to the south.	
GREEN LINE E. of TEMPLEUX LA FOSSE (A.1)	23-3-18		At midnight Mar 22/23 the Brigade moved forward from AIZECOURT LE HAUT to take its place in the GREEN LINE – E of GURLU WOOD (A.1). The move was completed by 3 a.m. Mar 23rd.	
			The enemy attacked along the whole GREEN LINE at 7.00 a.m. & broke through to the S. of TEMPLEUX. The right flank of the division was again left in the air & under heavy pressure the line fell back to the PERONNE – CAMBRAI ROAD – W of GURLU WOOD, where the enemy was held in check for some considerable time by rifle fire.	
			The continued advance of the enemy on PERONNE made a further withdrawal necessary and during the course of the morning, the line swung back to the neighbourhood of BOUCHAVESNES (AMIENS L.1)	
			During the night of Mar 23/24 the Battalion moved into a position N.E. of CLERY SUR SOMME (AMIENS K.1), the whole division being in the neighbourhood.	
N.E. of CLERY-SUR-SOMME MAUREPAS BRAY-SUR-SOMME	24-3-18		The morning of the 24th came with brilliant sunshine. The enemy made no attempt at a frontal attack on the positions held by the Division but large forces of hostile infantry could be seen from the direction of ALLAINES and MT ST QUENTIN (AMIENS L.1) towards CLERY-SUR-SOMME and it was realised that the enemy was again trying his outflanking tactics.	

A7092 Wt W125 g/M1293 750,000. 1/17. D. D & L., Ltd. Forms/C2118/14.

Instructions regarding War Diaries and Intelligence Summaries are contained in F. S. Regs., Part II. and the Staff Manual respectively. Title pages will be prepared in manuscript.

IX

WAR DIARY
or
INTELLIGENCE SUMMARY.

(*Erase heading not required.*)

Army Form C. 2118.

Place	Date	Hour	Summary of Events and Information	Remarks and references to Appendices
	24-3-18		Towards 11 a.m. a further withdrawal became necessary. CLERY-SUR-SOMME had fallen to the enemy who was pushing N from that village. At one period during the withdrawal the Battalion was in great danger of being entirely surrounded but owing to the magnificent working of a Lewis Gun by 2/Lt METTERS of D Company who inflicted severe casualties on the enemy, the Battalion was able to withdraw from a very critical situation.	
			During the afternoon the Brigade concentrated in MAUREPAS (AMIENS K1) and passed through a Brigade of the 35th Division, which had come up as a relieving Brigade.	
			At 4.30 p.m. orders were received to the effect that the Brigade would march to Bray sur Somme (AMIENS I.1). The Battalion arrived at BRAY about 8 p.m. and encamped W of the village.	
BRAY SUR SOMME CHIPILLY	25-3-18		In the afternoon of the 25th a composite company of 3 officers + 150 O.R. under the command of CAPT E.R. GREGORY M.C. left to join a composite Battalion under the command of MAJOR BURDETT, 6th Bn Leic Regt. The remainder of the Battalion proceeding to CHIPILLY (AMIENS H2) at 10 p.m.	
CHIPILLY BRESLE	26-3-18		On the morning of the 26th a second composite company of 3 officers and 150 O.R. under the command of CAPT PEMBERTON left to join a composite Battalion under the command of LT-COL MACULLOCH 9th KOYLI. The nucleus of the Battalion under MAJOR H.E.C. ANDERSON marched to BRESLE (AMIENS G.1) via SAILLY LAURETTE SAILLY-LE-SEC MERICOURT L'ABBE and RIBEMONT-SUR-ANCRE	
BRESLE VADENCOURT	27-3-18		During the morning of the 27th the nucleus of the Battalion moved to the CHATEAU at VADENCOURT (LENS 11. G.6) and came under the command of the B.G.C. 62nd Inf Bde.	

A7092 Wt. W12839/M1293 750,000 1/17 D. D. & L., Ltd. Forms/C2118/14.

Instructions regarding War Diaries and Intelligence Summaries are contained in F. S. Regs., Part II. and the Staff Manual respectively. Title pages will be prepared in manuscript.

WAR DIARY
or
INTELLIGENCE SUMMARY.
(Erase heading not required.)

Army Form C. 2118.

Place	Date	Hour	Summary of Events and Information	Remarks and references to Appendices
VADENCOURT	28th & 29th 3-18.		The nucleus of the Battalion under MAJOR H.E.L. ANDERSON remained at VADENCOURT during the 28th and 29th of March. The 2 Composite Companies were operating in the BRAY-CHIPILLY-MORLANCOURT-RIBEMONT AREA.	
ALLONVILLE	30-3-18.		The nucleus of the Battalion moved to ALLONVILLE (AMIENS E.) in the evening of March 30th and went into Billets in that village.	
ALLONVILLE	31-3-18.		The 2 Composite Companies rejoined the Battalion in the afternoon of the 31st & the Battalion was immediately reorganised and reformed into the 4 companies.	
			The following casualties were sustained by the Battalion during the heavy fighting brought about by the great German attack. Officers. LT-COL. A.T. LE M. UTTERSON DSO. Missing believed P. of W. 22-3-18. CAPT. H. SPENCER SMITH M.C. Missing believed P. of W. 22-3-18. CAPT. W. CARTER ~~2nd~~ R.A.M.C. Missing believed P. of W. 22-3-18. A Company LT. R.L. SENNETT. Wounded 22-3-18. 2/LT. V.G. MATTHEWS Wounded 21-3-18. 2/LT. EVANS Wounded 22-3-18. B Company LT. R.W. CALLISON. Wounded & Missing. 24-3-18 Believed P. of W. 2/LT. JACKSON - Missing 22-3-18. C Company 2/LT. W.G. SMITH - Missing believed Killed 21-3-18. 2/LT J. GEMMELL Wounded 22-3-18 ~~2/Lt ... Wounded~~, D Company CAPT. R.M.T. DAVISON Wounded & Missing 22-3-18. 2/LT. G.H. DOBSON wounded 21-3-18. 2/LT. E.R. HILL Wounded 21-3-18. 2/LT. W. DONE Wounded 22-3-18. 2/LT. W.H. SHAW Wounded 23-3-18.	
			Other Ranks Killed 28, Wounded 109, Gassed 4, Missing 260, Wounded and Missing 14.	
			Total - Officers 15 Other Ranks 415.	
			[illegible signature] Major Cmdg. 8th Battn Leic. Regt.	
			April 6th 1918	
			2353 Wt. W2544/1451 700,000 5/15 D. D. & L. A.D.S.S./Forms/C. 2118.	

Copy letter from A.J.FLETCHER. I.O. 8th Bn.Liecestershire Regiment.

THE FOG- MARCH 21st 1918.

Before replying to the four questions asked, it is necessary to state that I was not actually in the front line at the commencement of the attack. As Intelligence Officer of 8th Bn.Leicestershire Regiment, I was with Battalion Headquarters in the village of Epehy.

When the enemy bombardment began the village itself was enveloped in a dense fog, in which it was not possible to see more than 20 yards ahead, but it was not until after 8 a.m. that I went into the front line area under orders from the Commanding Officer.

(a) Between 8 a.m. and 9 a.m. the fog covered the whole of the 110th Brigade front, there can be no question of patches, as far as the Brigade front was concerned the fog was universal, it was particularly dence over our trenches on the right of "Fourteen Willows" Road.

(b) Between the times stated the utmost limit of visability was 70 yards ahead of 8th Battalion front line.

(c) The fog began to clear just after 10 a.m. when the sun became strong enough to break through; at 11 a.m. the fog lay in patches over the village, but was rapidly dispersing.

(d) By midday, when I was sent with a message to O.C.7th Battalion on our left, the fog had completely gone, the whole district being in brilliant sunshine.

(Sd) A. J. FLETCHER,

I.O. 8th Bn. Leis. Regt.

110th Brigade.

attd. 21st Division

1/8th BATTALION

LEICESTERSHIRE REGIMENT

APRIL 1918.

8th Battn The Leicestershire Regt

Instructions regarding War Diaries and Intelligence Summaries are contained in F. S. Regs., Part II. and the Staff Manual respectively. Title Pages will be prepared in manuscript.

April 1918

WAR DIARY
or
~~INTELLIGENCE~~ SUMMARY
(Erase heading not required.)

Army Form C. 2118.

Vol 31

Place	Date	Hour	Summary of Events and Information	Remarks and references to Appendices
ALLONVILLE	April 1st		On the morning of the 1st the Battalion received orders to entrain at ST. ROCH Station (NEAR AMIENS) at 1.30pm. The Battalion went by march route to the entraining Station.	
POPERINGHE	April 2nd		On the morning of the 2nd the Battalion detrained at HOPOUTRE (near POPERINGHE) + proceeded by lorries to MONMOUTHSHIRE CAMP (near DRANOUTRE)	
DRANOUTRE	April 4th		On the evening of the 4th/5th the Battalion moved up into Divisional Reserve. The Battalion was accomodated in KEMMEL SHELTERS CAMP (near KEMMEL)	
KEMMEL SHELTERS	April 7th		On the evening of the 7th/8th the Battalion received orders to move to CURRAGH CAMP (near WESTOUTRE)	
CURRAGH CAMP	April 8th		On the morning of the 8th the Battalion moved to ONTARIO CAMP (near RENINGHELST)	
ONTARIO CAMP	April 9th		On the afternoon of the 9th the Battalion received orders to move to MANAWATU CAMP (near ZILLEBEKE LAKE). The same evening the Battalion entrained at ZEVECOTEN (Light Railway Station) + relieved the Yorkshire Regiment at MANAWATU CAMP.	
MANAWATU CAMP	April 10th		At 5.0.am. on the 10th as a result of prisoners statements re pending attack the Battalion was ordered to move into close reserve to TORR TOP + CANADA TUNNELS in readiness The Battalion remained in this position until the 13th.	

2449 Wt. W14957/M90 750,000 1/16 J.B.C. & A. Forms/C.2118/12.

Instructions regarding War Diaries and Intelligence Summaries are contained in F. S. Regs., Part II. and the Staff Manual respectively. Title Pages will be prepared in manuscript.

WAR DIARY
or
INTELLIGENCE SUMMARY
(Erase heading not required.)

Army Form C. 2118.

Place	Date	Hour	Summary of Events and Information	Remarks and references to Appendices
CANADA TUNNELS	April 13th		On the evening of the 13th the Battalion took over the front line from the 6th Bn Leicestershire Regt. Dispositions as follows – Two Companies in the front line – one Company in Support – one Company in reserve. Battn H.Q. was situated in TORR TOP.	
TORR TOP.	April 15th		On the evening of the 15th the Battalion received orders to withdraw to the G.H.Q.1. line N & S. along YPRES – KRUISTRAATHOEK ROAD. The 6th Bn Leicestershire Regt covered this withdrawal & took up an outpost position along E edge of TORR TOP – MT. SORREL RIDGE – 1500 yards E of ZILLEBEKE. The Battalion was accomodated in FORRESTOR CAMP until the 16th & owing to Shelling moved into G.H.Q.1. trenches. Battn H.Q. was situated in SWAN CHATEAU	
G.H.Q.1. line of trenches.	April 18th		On the evening of the 18th/19th the Battalion took over the line of posts from the 6th Bn Leicestershire Regt. Dispositions as follows – one Company in BEDFORD HOUSE with outposts – one Company in WOODCOTE HOUSE with outposts – two Companies in G.H.Q.1 & 2. defensive lines. The enemy attacked on the 26th & the outpost line on TORR TOP was withdrawn – BEDFORD HOUSE line then became the front line. The enemy penetrated posts on the right of the Battalion & the Battalion filled in the gap as a defensive flank. on the 24th On the 28th the enemy attacked & captured VOORMEZEELE & LOCKS. again exposing the right of the Battalion. The gap was again filled by the Battalion.	

2449 Wt. W14957/M90 750,000 1/16 J.B.C. & A. Forms/C.2118/12.

Army Form C. 2118.

Instructions regarding War Diaries and Intelligence Summaries are contained in F. S. Regs., Part II. and the Staff Manual respectively. Title Pages will be prepared in manuscript.

WAR DIARY
or
INTELLIGENCE SUMMARY
(Erase heading not required.)

Place	Date	Hour	Summary of Events and Information	Remarks and references to Appendices
			The Battalion was relieved by the 9th Bn Welsh Regt (19th Division) & the line was handed over intact – no ground having been lost by the Battalion. The Battalion did twenty one days continuously in the line [illegible] Lt Col Cmdg. 6th Bn Leicestershire Regiment.	

2449 Wt. W14957/M90 750,000 1/16 J.B.C. & A. Forms/C.2118/12.

8th Bn The Leicestershire Regiment

Sheet 7

WAR DIARY 110/71

or

~~INTELLIGENCE SUMMARY~~

(Erase heading not required.)

Army Form C. 2118.

Instructions regarding ~~War Diaries and Intelligence~~ Summaries are contained in F. S. Regs., Part II. and the Staff Manual respectively. Title Pages will be prepared in manuscript.

Ref. map HAZEBROUCKE 5a 1/100,000
SOISSONS 1/40,000
BERRY-AU-BAC S.E. 1/10,000

Vol 32

Place	Date	Hour	Summary of Events and Information	Remarks and references to Appendices
near BUSSEBOOM.	1.5.18		On the morning of the 1st the Battalion went by march route to BOIS DE BEAUVOORDE - 500 yards N of the CASSEL - STEENVOORDE ROAD. The Battalion bivouaced there for the night.	
BOIS DE BEAUVOORDE	2.5.18		On the morning of the 2nd the Battalion proceeded by march route to BUYSSCHEURE via CASSEL - a long halt for dinners being taken just W of CASSEL. The Battalion was accomodated in a field in tents. The Battalion remained at BUYSSCHEURE for two days.	
BUYSSCHEURE	5.5.18		At 3.30 am on the morning of the 5th the Battalion left BUYSSCHEURE & proceeded by march route to WIZERNES via ST. OMER. The Battalion entrained there at 9am for the CHATEAU THIERRY area (E of PARIS).	
IN THE TRAIN	6.5.18	-	At 9pm on the evening of the 6th the Battalion detrained at BERZY-SAVIGNY & proceeded by march route to AOUGNY. The Battalion was accomodated in the village in billets. The Battalion remained in AOUGNY for 7 days - during which period - a set programme of training was carried out	
AOUGNY	13.5.18		On the afternoon of the 13th the Battalion proceeded by march route to PEVY where accomodation was found in huts & billets for the night.	
PEVY.	14.5.18		On the morning of the 14th at 3am the Battalion proceeded by march route to D CAMP - CHALONS DE VERGEUR (E of BOUVANCOURT). On this date the 110th Inf. Bde took over the Centre Brigade Sector of the Divisional front - this Battalion being in reserve at the above mentioned Camp. The Battalion remained in this Camp for six days - during which period a certain amount of training was carried out according to programme.	

2449 Wt. W14957/M90 750,000 1/16 J.B.C. & A. Forms/C.2118/12.

Sheet II

Army Form C. 2118.

Instructions regarding War Diaries and Intelligence Summaries are contained in F. S. Regs., Part II. and the Staff Manual respectively. Title Pages will be prepared in manuscript.

WAR DIARY
or
INTELLIGENCE SUMMARY

(Erase heading not required.)

Place	Date	Hour	Summary of Events and Information	Remarks and references to Appendices
CHALONS DE VERGEUR	20.5.18		On the evening of the 20th the Battalion took over the right Subsector of the Centre brigade from the 6th Bn Leicestershire Regiment. Dispositions as follows – A Coy right front Company – B Coy – left front Company – C Coy right Support Coy D Coy – left Support Company. The Battalion front ran about 1000 yards E of the AISNE – MARNE canal between CAUROY + CORMICY. There were six lines of defence between front line + CAUROY – CORMICY ROAD. The 1st + 2nd lines were within the front Coy area. The 3rd + 4th lines were just W of CANAL along W edge of LAON – RHEIMS ROAD. The 5th line ran through Battn HQ about 700 yards W of CANAL + the 6th line just E of CAUROY – CORMICY ROAD.	
			The 3rd + 4th lines were within Support Coy area. The 5th line was held by Battalion H.Q.	
			An inter platoon relief took place after 3 days in the line + on completion of six days in the line an inter Company relief was ordered.	
FRONT LINE	26.6.18		During the period the Battalion had been in the line up to the 26th the hostile artillery activity had been very slight – Much movement had been reported behind the enemy lines + the French Authorities were of the opinion that an attack was to be expected on the Divisional front.	
			At 9.30pm on the night of the 26th when the inter Coy relief was in progress, a message was received from Brigade that from two prisoners statements	

2449 Wt. W14957/M90 750,000 1/16 J.B.C. & A. Forms/C.2118/12.

Sheet II

Instructions regarding War Diaries and Intelligence Summaries are contained in F. S. Regs., Part II. and the Staff Manual respectively. Title Pages will be prepared in manuscript.

WAR DIARY
or
INTELLIGENCE SUMMARY
(Erase heading not required.)

Army Form C. 2118.

Place	Date	Hour	Summary of Events and Information	Remarks and references to Appendices
			(captured that night) the enemy intended to attack along whole AISNE front including the front held by the Division – Bombardment to commence at 1am, the attack at 3 am. This statement proved to be correct for punctually at 1.am. the enemy put down a heavy barrage on the Divisional area. The back areas were shelled with gas shells chiefly – the mustard type being mostly used. The forward area was not subjected to gas as much as the back areas (i.e in rear of Batt. H.Q).	
			From the time the barrage opened all communications were cut + approximately at 5.30am a runner reported having been attacked by a German in the 3rd line W of the Canal. At 6 am the enemy were seen from Batt. H.Q. to be advancing in small parties across the Canal. By this time a platoon from the Battalion NUCLEUS party had arrived to reinforce, + 2 platoons from the 9th Bn Leicestershire Regiment + a second platoon from the Battalion NUCLEUS were on their way. The four platoons comprised the NUCLEUS Coy under MAJOR H.C. TYLER. M.C 9th Batt.	
			A verbal message was sent to Brigade that no news had been received from any Company + that the Battalion was holding the 5th line 400x W of the Canal. This message reached Brigade at 9am.	
			At 8.30am the LEFT Support Company Commander (LIEUT R.H GRAVER) reported at Batt. H.Q. with 12 men – the RIGHT SUPPORT Company Commander (LIEUT A. HALKYARD) reported also a little later with 50 men – most of whom were stragglers from other Battalions. These 50 men were used to continue the line S. of Batt. H.Q. A block was established in each Communication	

Shut IV

Army Form C. 2118.

WAR DIARY
or
INTELLIGENCE SUMMARY
(Erase heading not required.)

Instructions regarding War Diaries and Intelligence Summaries are contained in F. S. Regs., Part II. and the Staff Manual respectively. Title Pages will be prepared in manuscript.

Place	Date	Hour	Summary of Events and Information	Remarks and references to Appendices
			trench forward of the line & small posts were established behind these blocks. This was in accordance with instructions received meanwhile from Brigade. The three NUCLEUS platoons above mentioned had arrived by this time & this line was held for some hours by the NUCLEUS Company plus the mixed force under Lt. A. HALKYARD & the Battn. H.Q. L.G. platoon.	
			Battn. H.Q. moved back to a position just E of the CAUROY - CORMICY ROAD in a communication trench. The Battn. H.Q. details & the remainder of the LEFT Support Company being used as support to the front line took up a position there also.	
			During the whole of this time the hostile artillery was barraging all communication trenches, roads & tracks forward from Brigade very heavily.	
			A Company (Capt SCHOLES) of the 6th Bn Leicestershire Regiment came up to reinforce the Battalion at about 3pm & held the 6th line just E of the CAUROY CORMICY ROAD.	
			A report came through that the enemy had entered our trenches on the left of the 5th line & that they were bombing their way towards the main communication trench leading to the CAUROY CORMICY ROAD. It was also reported that the enemy were using flammenwerfer. When the NUCLEUS Company under Major H.C. TYLER. M.C. was forced out of the 5th line they withdrew down the C.T. to the 6th line leaving a platoon to form a block just W of the junction of the C.T. & the 5th line of resistance. This block was held for some hours by 12 men of this Battalion.	
			Battn. H.Q. moved back to a position 100x S.W of the CAUROY CORMICY ROAD	

2449 Wt. W14957/M90 750,000 1/16 J.B.C. & A. Forms/C.2118/12.

Sheet V

Instructions regarding War Diaries and Intelligence Summaries are contained in F. S. Regs., Part II. and the Staff Manual respectively. Title pages will be prepared in manuscript.

WAR DIARY
or
INTELLIGENCE SUMMARY.
(Erase heading not required.)

Army Form C. 2118.

Place	Date	Hour	Summary of Events and Information	Remarks and references to Appendices
			Two more Coys of the 6th Battalion Leicestershire Regiment came up to reinforce the one Coy holding the 6th line. This made the garrison of the 6th line – 3 Coys of the 6th Battn plus a mixed force of about 30 men under Lieut Graves. Major Tyler's Company which now numbered about 50 men was withdrawn into support of the 6th line in wood W of the CAUROY – CORMICY ROAD.	
			Battalion HQ. was forced to move back owing to the enemy having pushed forward machine guns ~~forward~~ in the wood S W of the CAUROY CORMICY ROAD	
			By this time the Battalion consisted of 1 platoon (HQ platoon) + Battn HQ.	
			As the line was now held by 3 Coys of the 6th Bn Leic Regt with 1 Coy of 6th Bn Leic Regt in support near LA TUILERIE plus Major Tyler's NUCLEUS Coy, Lt Col CHANCE Commanding the 6th Bn Leic Regt took over Command of the Battalion front at 8.0pm. Bn H.Q. then withdrew to Bde HQ + moved back with Bde HQ. to VAUX VARENNES	
			Elements of the Battalion numbering 4 officers + about 50 men remained under Lt Col Chance who commanded the Composite Battn consisting of the three battalions in the Brigade.	
			During the night of 27th/28th Lt Col Chance's force took up a position N of VAUX VARENNES but was withdrawn at 3.0 am on the 28th + took up a new position on the high ground S.E of VAUX VARENNES	
			Rations for the 28th were issued at this position.	

(A7092). Wt. W12839/M1293. 750,000. 1/17. D. D. & L., Ltd. Forms/C. 2118/14.

Sheet VI

Instructions regarding War Diaries and Intelligence Summaries are contained in F. S. Regs., Part II. and the Staff Manual respectively. Title pages will be prepared in manuscript.

WAR DIARY
or
INTELLIGENCE SUMMARY.
(Erase heading not required.)

Army Form C. 2118.

Place	Date	Hour	Summary of Events and Information	Remarks and references to Appendices
			The enemy attacked & drove line back at about 8 am. [illegible] when Brigade received orders to go in Reserve at PEVY. The enemy however had approached PEVY from the N W & so a general withdrawal was carried out to HILL E of PROUILLY where a line was organised & held till about 12 ~~midnight~~ noon.	
			French troops then took over the line & British troops of all brigades withdrew to S. side of the VESLE where the Division took up a line from LES VENTES – BRANSCOURT inclusive	
			Troops were sorted out into Brigades – troops of the 110th Inf Bde under Lt Col SAWYER Commanding the 9th Bn Leic Regt held the centre sector from TILE WORKS to about 1000 yards W of this.	
			The enemy attacking from the west pushed their line back to heights N of ROSNAY during the afternoon of the 29th	
			H.Q. 6th Battn was to relieve COL SAWYER on the night of the 29th/30th but orders were received that the French had taken over the line & that British troops would withdraw to POURCY.	
			The withdrawal of the Brigade troops was complete by 4 a.m. the 30th	
POURCY	30.5.18		On the morning of the 30th the Battn moved by march route to FORET D EPERNAY ~~CORMOYEUX~~ & bivouaced in a field close to the wood	
FORET D EPERNAY ~~CORMOYEUX~~	31.5.18		On the morning of the 31st the Battalion moved by march route to ETRECHY & was accomodated in billets there	

H Cortland Anderson Major Comdg 6th Bn Leic Regt

(A7092). Wt. W12839/M1293. 750,000. 1/17. D. D. & L., Ltd. Forms/C.2118/14.

www.ingramcontent.com/pod-product-compliance
Lightning Source LLC
Chambersburg PA
CBHW081355160426
43192CB00013B/2417